Agnieszka Legutko-Ołownia

Kraków's Kazimierz

Town of Partings and Returns

Wydawnictwo Bezdroża B

Cooperation: Dominika Zaręba (concept and text of *Route 5*)

Series: *Towns and districts*, cycle: *genius loci*
Concept of the cycle: Dominika Zaręba, Łukasz Galusek, Tomasz Ostrowski
Editorial Work: Marzena Daszewska, Łukasz Galusek
Proofreaders: Søren Gauger, Scotia Gilroy
Photographs: Dominika Zaręba
The book contains reproductions of oil paintings depicting Kazimierz by Iwona Siwek-Front
of the "Town and People" series (www.spam.art.pl/front, e-mail: iwka_sfront@wp.pl)
Cartographic and diagram editors: Marzena Daszewska, Łukasz Galusek
Maps: Bartłomiej Kuniczuk, Bartłomiej Cisowski (cooperation)
Graphic design: Kuba Sowiński, Łukasz Galusek (cooperation)
Typesetting: Paweł Kosmalski, Paweł Panczakiewicz
Print: Drukarnia SKLENIARZ, Kraków

The authors and the publisher of this guidebook have made every effort to provide the most accurate
information. Nevertheless, they cannot take responsibility for any consequences arising from the use
of information provided herein. We would appreciate if our readers called our attention to any errors
or outdated information, thanks to which we shall be able to correct future editions.
Please contact us at the following address:

Wydawnictwo Bezdroża
ul. Pychowicka 7, 30-364 Kraków
tel.: (0-12) 269 29 61, 267 77 10, fax: (0-12) 267 77 11
e-mail: biuro@bezdroza.com.pl, http://www.bezdroza.com.pl

Distribution to bookstores and wholesale outlets only via the "Amistad" Trade Office
tel.: (0-12) 267 77 10, fax: (0-12) 267 77 11, e-mail: biuro@amistad.pl

First Edition, Kraków 2004
ISBN 83-89676-11-7
Copyright by Wydawnictwo Bezdroża, 2004

Genius loci
The spirit of a place dwells in both stones and people. Mysterious, it inspires quests.
At times it demands the patience of an archaeologist, at other times reacts to an artistic
provocation. Various paths lead to it: records of the past, works of art, colours, scents and sounds.
No one knows its mystery, but many derive spiritual satisfaction from communing with it.
This cycle of guidebooks is addressed to all who wish to read the text of the town.
(Editors of Bezdroża)

CONTENTS

Farewell, my Kraków!

Fare thee well,
The cart is hitched up,
Waiting in front of my house.
The savage enemy drives me cruelly from you
As one would drive away a dog.

   Farewell, my Kraków!
   Perhaps today is the last day
   I will ever see everything dear to me.
At my mother's grave,
I cried out my heart.
It was hard to part from her.
I cried my eyes out, until the last tear
Wetted my father's cold stone.
I couldn't find my grandfather's grave.
His gravestone must have turned to dust by now.

   Farewell, my Kraków!
   Holy is your ground.
   My parents rest in it.
   I am not destined to lie next to them;
   A grave awaits me somewhere far away
Farewell, my Kraków!
Fare thee well!
The cart is hitched up.
Waiting in front of my house
The savage enemy drives me away from you,
cruelly,
As one would drive away a dog.

Mordechai Gebirtig (transl. Manfred Lemm)

בלײַב געזונט מיר קראָקע!
בלײַבזשע מיר געזונט.
ס־װאָרט די פֿור געשפּאַנט שױן פֿאַר מײַן הױז,
מ־טרײַבט דער װילדער שׂונא
װי מ־טרײַבט אַ הונט
מיט אכזריות מיך פֿון דיר אַרױס...
בלײַבט געזונט מיר קראָקע
איך זע אפֿשר הײַנט
ס־לעצטס מאָל מיט אַלץ װאָס ליב איז מיר,
אױף מײַן מאמעס קבֿר
ס־האַרץ זיך אױסגעװײנט
אױסגעװײנט די אױגן
ביז דער לעצטער טרער,
באַנעצט מיט זײ דעם מאַמענס קאַלטן שטײן
כ־האָב דעם זײדענס קבֿר
נישט געפֿונען מער
עס מוז שױן זאַמד פֿון זײַן מצבֿה זײַן...
בלײַב געזונט מיר קראָקע
הײליק איז דײַן ערד.
מאַטע־מאַמע רוען דאָ אין איר
לעבן זײ צו ליגן
איז מיר נישט באַשערט
ס־װאָרט אַ קבֿר ערגעץ װײַט אױף מיר...
בלײַב געזונט מיר קראָקע!
בלײַבזשע מיר געזונט,
ס־װאָרט די פֿור שױן געשפּאַנט פֿאַר מײַן הױז
ס־טרײַבט דער װילדער שׂונא
װי מען טרײַבט אַ הונט
מיט אכזריות פֿון דיר אַרױס....
קראָקע 24 אָקטאָבער 1940

If not here – then where?...
If not now – then when?...
(Janusz Makuch and Krzysztof Gierat)

INTRODUCTION

The town of Kazimierz is inseparably bound with the history of the Kraków Jews, and is intrinsically connected with Kraków. The relationship of Jews with Kazimierz and Kraków is sometimes referred to as "the phenomenon of expulsion and return".

Jews settled in the centre of Kraków most likely in the second half of the 12th century in the vicinity of present-day St Ann Street. They lived there until the middle of the 15th century, only to move into the vicinity of present-day Szczepański Square and remain there until 1495, when they were expelled from Kraków. Interestingly, the very first mention of the name Kraków (Karako) comes from a Jewish merchant and diplomat, Ibrahim ibn Jakub, who in 965 visited Prague and Kraków on his way to Germany and Moravia on a diplomatic mission from a Spanish Caliph.

Although Jews settled in Kazimierz, they remained closely connected with Kraków, where Jewish shops and workshops were located. Thus, as a distinguished Jewish historian, Majer Bałaban wrote: "A Kraków Jew had two quarters; in one he lived, he prayed, he raised children, in the other he worked; ... and the way the Jew passed every day from Kazimierz to Kraków constituted a division between a Jew-human and a Jew-merchant or broker".

Only after 1800, when Kazimierz became formally annexed to Kraków, and especially after 1867, when Jews were granted equal citizenship rights, did they begin to settle all over Kraków.

The Jews living in Kazimierz regarded themselves as the 'Kraków' Jews, which may be illustrated by inscriptions on the tombstones at the Remuh Cemetery, where the name of Kazimierz does not appear once, while the name of Kraków appears a number of times; they were also referred to in such a way in non-Jewish documents.

In 1940 when Mordechai Gebirtig, a famous Jewish bard living in Kazimierz, shared the fate of other Kraków Jews and was expelled, he wrote a touching goodbye-song called *Farewell, my Kraków* (Blayb gezunt mir, Kroke).

After 1989 the wave of returns began; in 1993 Steven Spielberg filmed *Schindler's List* here, marking Kraków and Kazimierz on the tourist map of the world. An event which brings thousands of Jews and non-Jews from all over the world every year is the Jewish Culture Festival. All come here to submerge themselves in the magnificent world of Jewish music, arts, tradition, history and culture – the world that is no longer present in everyday Kazimierz.

What distinguishes this town is the former coexistence of Christians and Jews: where else can we stop at the crossroads of Rabbi Meisels and Corpus Christi Streets? But the genuine treasure of Kazimierz is its vitality, which lives and surprises with new images despite the previous desolation: it is here that the artistic and social pulse of Kraków races; in this space, like in no other, artistic souls conjure nostalgia, emotion and ironic anecdote. In other words: Central Europe! A performance, concert, twilight, coffee and conversation have their unique taste. This guidebook will give you a hint how to find it, for body and for soul.

ABOUT THE AUTHOR

Agnieszka Legutko-Ołownia is a graduate of the English Department at the Jagiellonian University in Kraków, a translator, a tour guide in Kazimierz and Kraków and is passionate about foreign languages, culture and history. Her interest in Jewish culture began around ten years ago and soon turned into a great fascination. Soon afterwards she 'discovered' Kazimierz – 'recovering from the ordeal of divorcing communism' – which she immediately fell in love with. She has been giving guided tours for five years to foreign guests, mainly of Jewish origin, who very often turn out to be a rich source of knowledge and incredible stories written by life. She has also been taking active part in the Jewish Culture Festival for the last few years (as an interpreter and, as in 2003, a tour guide to the ghetto on the last day of the Festival), she has been learning Yiddish (in her MA dissertation she compared the original of a short story by Isaac Bashevis Singer, "The Last Demon", with its Polish and English translations), and at present she wishes to extend her knowledge of Jewish culture, literature and history through doctoral studies.

History

FOUNDATION OF KAZIMIERZ

The charming town of Kazimierz, named after its founder and benefactor King Kazimierz Wielki (Casimir the Great) (1333-70), was established in 1335 on the site of three settlements: St Michael's Church on Skałka [the Rock] dating from the 11th century, and the no longer existing St Jacob's Church and St Laurent's Church, as well as the village of Bawół, annexed in 1340.

In the 14th century the island-town of Kazimierz had the shape of an irregular quadrangle with dimensions of 900 m x 500 m, about 45 hectares. In the middle of the 14th century Kazimierz and its outskirts were inhabited by 1,500-2,000 people.

Historian Karol Estreicher writes: "The town was surrounded by walls, the streets were laid out, the main market square was marked and foundations, thanks to the king's generosity, were laid for two new churches. The population that had settled here was Polish, unlike the more German-dominated Kraków. The town was entirely independent of Kraków".

Kazimierz, like Kraków, was endowed with the Magdeburg Law, according to which markets were held every Thursday, and burghers of Kazimierz had the right to trade in Kraków, flume timber, possess the cloth hall and the cloth shearing hall, as well as to transport beer and liquor. The market square laid out in Kazimierz (present-day Wolnica Square) was 195 m x 195 m, only slightly smaller than the Kraków Market Square (200 m x 200 m).

The Kazimierz Market Square was originally four-fold greater than present-day Wolnica Square – it stretched to ul. Augustiańska, Węgłowa and Trynitarska. In the middle of the market, there was a town hall and a cloth hall consisting of 25 stalls, and in the western part of the market there also stood mostly wooden stalls.

Ul. Krakowska [Street] has been the main street of Kazimierz until now. The city walls were guarded by four gates: from the north, where Dietla and Krakowska streets cross, there was the Clay Gate; from the south, at the crossroads of ul. Krakowska and Podgórska – the Salt Gate; from the west – the Skawińska Gate and the Cattle Gate, according to some sources located in the vicinity of present-day ul. Szeroka, but other sources have identified it with the Bocheńska Gate, located at the end of present-day ul. Gazowa. Kazimierz was accessible only through bridges leading to the gates, although there also used to be gateways in the walls (e.g. a Jewish gateway is mentioned in 1386 and 1389).

KING CASIMIR'S PLANS

King Casimir the Great established Kazimierz as a rival town to Kraków, which he did not favour much, and perhaps intended it to become the main centre of the united monarchy and the future university town. According to chronicler Jan Długosz: "King Casimir wished to elevate and enhance his realm with *studium generale*, following the example of other countries, in the town of Kazimierz, and single-handedly founded adjacent Kraków, … near the city wall, in a vast area stretching around for more than 1,000 steps, he built a sightly-shaped new university, pretty houses, chambers, lecture rooms and numerous apartments for doctors and masters of the school, which he had built of stone. … The university nonetheless faced adversities after the king's death, and its foundation and endowment was never realised".

Therefore, the intended campus of the oldest university in Poland and the second-oldest in Central Europe (after the University of Prague), the Jagiellonian University, was not established in Kazimierz; instead, two monumental Gothic churches were erected at the king's initiative: the St Catherine and St Margaret's Church and the Corpus Christi Church which have proudly overlooked Kazimierz until now. King Casimir, concerned for the town's spiritual development, brought the Hermit Friars of Saint Augustine from Prague in 1342 and founded a monastery at St Catherine and Margaret's Church for them. He also erected a Gothic church on Skałka, but there is little information about it.

To recapitulate, one may say that Kazimierz was designed with great panache. It obtained numerous privileges, public utility buildings, such as a town hall, cloth hall, hospital, two new churches and a monastery, and above all, grounds for a university. Although the king's death brought some of his projects to a halt, Kazimierz prospered till the first half of the 17th century. The area of Kazimierz constituted 2/3 of Kraków's area. In the Middle Ages it was one of the most important Polish towns, and almost as wealthy as nearby Kraków.

In 1495 Jews expelled from Kraków settled here, and the *Oppidum Judaeorum*, 'the Jewish town', came into being. Since then, Kazimierz has been a town of two cultures – Christian and Jewish.

THE JEWISH QUARTER IN KRAKÓW

Let us go back to the second half of the 12th century when Jews began to arrive in Kraków. Jews had often sought refuge here from persecutions, increased during the Crusades – Crusaders never missed an opportunity to murder Jewish settlers they met on the way.

A historical record from 1304 tells us that Jewish houses, shops and businesses were located in the vicinity of *Judengasse*, Jewish Street in Kraków (now St Ann Street). As described by

King Casimir Greets the Jews

Majer Bałaban, the author of the first major history of the Kraków Jews: "in the 14th and 15th centuries there were two synagogues, a *kahal* house, bathhouse (mentioned in 1358), a school and a wedding house. ... On the corner of St Ann (Jewish) and Jagiellonian Streets there was an old synagogue overlooking a small square. In the middle of that square ... Jewish markets were held".

Another great wave of Jewish refugee immigration took place in the 14th century as a result of the Black Death, which swept across Europe between 1348 and 1351, during which 1/3 of the European population died (according to N. Davis around 30 mln people). The Plague was another reason for strong persecutions of Jews who were accused of causing it by, for example, poisoning the wells.

Casimir the Great is associated with the Jewish arrival in Poland, which can be seen in the bas-relief *King Casimir Greets the Jews* by Henryk Hochman at the former Kazimierz town hall in Wolnica Square. What is more, the king remained in Jewish memory as the most gracious ruler, which is evidenced by the 'Prayer of the Kraków Jews for their King' that has been preserved in the Kupa Synagogue.

SOCIAL STATUS OF JEWS

Another reason why Jews so eagerly settled in Kraków was the benevolence of King Casimir the Great towards them; the friendly attitude of the king has prevailed in tradition for many years.

King Casimir, the only Polish ruler called "the Great", was deemed a wise politician, a skilful diplomat, a patron of the arts, and above all a great economist who recognised the advantages of Jewish settlement in Poland. He managed to establish an efficient administration, a code of laws and a peaceful foreign policy, which allowed the dynamic economic growth of the country. He welcomed Jewish settlers, hoping to profit from their financial and commercial expertise. Jews assisted him in raising the country from economic ruin and bringing it nearer to Western European civilization.

Jews were repeatedly employed by Polish rulers as mint administrators and mint masters, which is evidenced by unilateral silver coins with Polish and Hebrew inscriptions dating from the 12th and 13th centuries.

In the second year of his reign, in 1335, King Casimir confirmed the Kalisz Privilege (granted to Jews by Boleslaw the Chaste in 1264) for the Kraków Jews, and in 1364 and 1367 he extended it to Jews all over Poland. The privilege made Jews subject to royal, not municipal, jurisdiction, permitted them to lend money on interest and mortgage, and guaranteed personal freedom and religious autonomy.

Jewish entrepreneurs were closely associated with the king. The best example of a powerful financial tycoon was Lewko, court banker of King Casimir the Great. According to Bałaban: "Lewko had grown into a top-class capitalist of his time in royal circles under the attentive care of King Casimir the Great, whom he undoubtedly remunerated generously. ... The king defended the rights of 'his Jew' and assisted him in collecting his debts. ... In 1368 the king ... entrusted Lewko with the administration of the royal salt-mines of Wieliczka and Bochnia, and the Mint of Kraków".

Lewko's clientele included nobility and clergy, as well as local gentry and townspeople. After his death in 1395 it took several decades to collect all the debts owed, and in order to commemorate such a remarkable banker one of the streets in Kazimierz was named after him. Jews contributed to the country's prosperity as merchants, craftsmen and bankers. However, their thrift and efficiency were a thorn in the side of Christian townspeople, who began to complain about Jews and attempted to impose various restrictions, e.g. bans on trading and mortgaging real estate. The economic success awakened active hatred in burghers, which resulted in anti-Jewish riots in the 14th century, often based on alleged blood libels and desecration of the host. The mob outbreaks were often initiated by debtors hoping to avoid paying off their debts (1407 and 1423), or fanatical preachers (like the Franciscan John of Capistrano in 1453). Jews were repeatedly accused of setting fires (e.g. in 1454). The disaster of 1485 forced Jews to relinquish the right to trade in Kraków "of their own free will".

In the meantime King Wladyslaw Jagiello restored the Academy of Kraków, and contrary to King Casimir's plans he erected university buildings on Jewish Street. In 1469 the Jews had to "voluntarily" evacuate the street on which the university was located, relinquish their buildings (two synagogues, a bath house, hospitals) to the university and move to present-day Szczepański Square, where they remained till 1495, when a fire broke out in a Jewish street and spread to Christian streets, leading King John Albert to expel the Jews from Kraków.

Therefore, on the site of the first Jewish quarter the university quarter had been established. According to Bałaban: "The Academy of Kraków erected its main building following the demolition or alteration of an old synagogue" (nowadays Collegium Maius lies in the heart of the former Jewish quarter); and on the site of an intended university campus a Jewish town had been established, exactly the opposite of King Casimir's plans.

DEVELOPMENT OF THE JEWISH TOWN IN KAZIMIERZ

The Jewish newcomers settled in the north-east part of Kazimierz, which from then on began to develop into the 'Jewish town'. The Jewish community in Kazimierz was already well-established at that time. Jews expelled from Prague in 1389, as well as the refugees from a Kraków pogrom in 1407, most likely took refuge here. There was a synagogue, nowadays called the Old Synagogue, and a cemetery. A new stage in the history of Kazimierz began.

Originally Jews occupied a small area near the Old Synagogue and the city wall. After the pestilence in 1551-52, which took the lives of 220 people, and due to lack of space in the previous cemetery (now the tiny square enclosed by a fence in the northern part of ul. Szeroka) the new Remuh Cemetery was established.

In 1553 an official agreement to the extension of the Jewish town was signed. The area was to be enclosed by a wall and a wooden fence, and three gates were to lead into the town: the main gate at present-day ul. Józefa 36, one in the wall near the Old Synagogue, and the only one preserved till now in the cemetery wall in ul. Jakuba.

Other agreements between the Jewish community and the municipality of Kazimierz in 1583 and 1608 led to expansion of the Jewish area from ul. Krakowska to ul. Szeroka. After the 1640s the borders remained unchanged for the next 200 years. The Jewish town was enclosed by walls built along the Kazimierz city walls from the north-east (now ul. Miodowa, Starowiślna and Dajwór), along ul. Bożego Ciała from the west and ul. św. Wawrzyńca and Józefa from the south. After 1583 only one gate (at the crossroads of ul. Józefa and Jakuba) led to the town.

Nevertheless, despite these expansions – according to the invaluable Bałaban – "the place inhabited by Jews was cramped", since apart from the natural population increase, still more and more Jews from Bohemia, Moravia, Italy, Spain and Portugal took refuge in Kazimierz. Therefore the original population of the Kraków Jews, who were Ashkenazic Jews from France and Germany, were joined by Sephardic Jews arriving from Spain and Portugal, who established their own community and prayer houses in Kazimierz.

Although Jews inhabited 1/5 of the whole Kazimierz area, they had shops and workshops all over Kazimierz. In 1570 the population of the Jewish town numbered 2,000, and between 1590 and 1640 it grew to about 5,000.

The Jewish community had an organised structure: it was presided over by a rabbi who, together with *kahal*, the community board, wielded power in the Jewish town. The rabbi supervised judicial, religious and educational sectors of life (e.g. performed marriages, granted divorces and excommunicated members of the community). Other important members of the community included the rector of *yeshiva*, the Talmudic university, the *hazan*, the cantor officiating in the synagogue and the *shohet*, the ritual slaughterer.

Christian-Jewish relations in Kazimierz were moderate, although Jews were frequently attacked by the Kraków students. In addition, students extorted special payments from Jews known as *kozubalec*. Traditional antagonisms were based on the commercial competition between Christian and Jewish merchants. Despite various restrictions imposed by Christian merchants and craftsmen, Jews engaged greatly in national and international trade and crafts.

In the 16th and 17th centuries Jews frequently traded in wax, honey, hides, salt, fish, and haberdashery; they imported cloth, silk, wine, paper and steel. As craftsmen they were not admitted to Christian guilds, so they could offer more attractive lower prices. This led Christian craftsmen such as tailors, furriers, butchers, weavers, bookbinders, goldsmiths and so on to complain about the Jewish competition. The Kraków Jews developed commercial ties with Prague, Silesia, Leipzig, Frankfurt, Warsaw, Gdańsk, and with Hungary, Vienna and Venice.

It needs to be mentioned that although Jews were transferred to Kazimierz and were inefficiently banned from trading in Kraków, the Kazimierz Jews were customarily drawn to Kraków. They maintained commerce there, and some individuals still lived there, for Kraków remained a flourishing trade centre, offering more profit opportunities than Kazimierz, which despite the king's intentions had never obtained such privileges as would have allowed it to effectively compete with Kraków.

Renaissance windows of the Canons' monastery

THE GOLDEN AGE OF CHRISTIAN KAZIMIERZ...

The 16th and the first half of the 17th century was a period of flourishing prosperity in Kazimierz, both Christian and Jewish. The (more than) 'golden age' meant not only a dynamic economic growth, but also cultural, scientific and architectural achievement, with the Renaissance in the background.

In the 15th century in the south-west, Christian part of Kazimierz a monastery was raised for the Canons Regular of Saint Augustine, brought here by King Wladyslaw Jagiello in 1405, who settled at the Corpus Christi Church. In 1412 the Canons took over the Corpus Christi parish and they have ministered to the Christian population of Kazimierz ever since. The church itself underwent significant alterations under the command of the active parish priest Marcin Kłoczyński (1612-44).

Jan Długosz, chronicler and tutor of the royal sons, brought the Pauline order (Friars of Saint Paul the Hermit) in 1472 who settled on Skałka, which since the middle of the 13th century had been a pilgrimage destination for both the country people and the rulers of the world. The Paulines, who were in charge of the church, erected a wooden monastery, which in the 16th century was rebuilt in stone. Długosz himself was buried there in 1480, and 400 years later the place had became the National Pantheon of great contributors to Polish culture. Since the

Middle Ages, an annual ceremonious procession from Wawel Cathedral to Skałka has taken place on 8th May, attended by nearly the entire Kraków clergy and townspeople, in honour of St Stanislaus the Bishop Martyr.

Kazimierz was a home to distinguished artists (a group of Italian architects settled here), such as Mateo Gucci, Thomas de Robore, Antonio Morosi, Alexander Gucci and Giovanni Battista Falconi, who not only beautifully ornamented the St Catherine and Corpus Christi Churches, but also influenced the appearance of the two synagogues and Kazimierz as a whole, where two-storey buildings and mansions (the Landau mansion, once belonging to the Jordans family, at ul. Szeroka 2) appeared. Bartolomeo Berecci, who created the famous Sigismund Chapel at Wawel Cathedral, also had his workshop here.

In 1527 Kazimierz was endowed with a water supply, which greatly improved the sanitary conditions of the town. In addition, a sewage system was implemented and a public bath house established which functioned till the 19th century.

...AND JEWISH KAZIMIERZ

By the first half of the 17th century five more synagogues had been erected in Kazimierz: the Remuh (1553-56), the High (1556-63), Popper (1620), Isaac (1638-1644) and finally the Kupa Synagogue (1635-47). The Old Synagogue burnt down and was rebuilt in Renaissance style by a distinguished Italian architect, Mateo Gucci. Three synagogues – the Old, the Remuh and Popper Synagogues – were located in ul. Szeroka, which did not happen anywhere else in Europe. The golden age in the Jewish town manifested itself not only in learning and scholarship, but also in administration and economic growth.

At the turn of the 15th and 16th centuries Jakub Polak, the first royally appointed rabbi of Kraków, settled in Kazimierz and in 1503 founded the first yeshiva, whose fame spread all over the world attracting many foreigners, who came to study here.

Kazimierz hosted the elite of Jewish scholars, such as Rabbi Moses Isserles (1510-72), known as Remuh, the most famous rabbi of Kraków, head of the Great Yeshiva of Kraków, and a codifier who, by adding notes on Ashkenazi customs in a work called Mappa [The Tablecloth], to a code of laws called *Shulhan Arukh* [The Laid Table] by the Sephardi codifier Joseph Karo, made it an authoritative guide for Orthodox Jews down to the present day (see p. 52). Another important figure of the time was the head of the Yeshiva of Kraków, Nathan Nata Spira (1583-1633), also called Megalle Amukkot after the title of his work – miracle-maker and the first lecturer on Jewish mysticism – Kabala (see box, p. 59). We cannot avoid mentioning Joel Sirkes (1561-1640), known as BaH, an abbreviation of *Beit-Hadash* [The New

House], a Kraków rabbi and one of the greatest Talmudic scholars of Poland. Another rabbi that needs to be mentioned was Gershon Saul Jom Tov Lipman Heller (1579-1654), best known for his commentaries to *Mishna*, called *Tosefot Yom Tov* (hence his name), by which he made a name for himself as an extraordinary scholar. All of them are buried in the Remuh Cemetery, which only adds to its uniqueness.

Nathan Hannover, a well-known Jewish historian, wrote: "We need no proof that in no other place among the Dispersion of the Israelites was there as much learning as in Poland. There were *yeshivas* in each and every community".

Having mentioned the great Jewish scholars, we cannot ignore a specific 'terminological schizophrenia' which appears in all sources – although we are in Kazimierz and we refer to Kazimierz, we talk about Kraków: e.g. rabbi of Kraków, the first Kabala lecturer in Kraków, etc.

The beginning of the 16th century is also associated with Hebrew printing, first introduced in 1534 by the Halicz brothers. The first book published in Yiddish (1534) was a popular glossary of the Bible, *Mirkewet-ha-Miszne* by Asher Anchel of Kraków.

The period of Jewish prosperity in Kazimierz was also due to King Sigismund Augustus's support, who – according to Bałaban – "came

Szmuel (Samuel), Aszer and Eliakim Halicz were the founders of the **first Hebrew printing house** in Poland. In 1537 the three brothers converted to Christianity. "Their products were immediately boycotted by their former co-religionists, who refused to buy from the converts ... and to pay off their debts" – reports Bałaban. "Then the neophytes entreated the king to force the Jewish communities in Kraków and Poznań to buy the entire stock of Hebrew books outright"; to which Sigismund the Old assented. An inventory of the impressive stock of 3,350 volumes was made, and in 1539 the first Hebrew printing house in Poland ceased to exist.

to the defence of Jews, whenever mob emotions prevailed, ... he assisted to protect their property, ... [therefore] Jews looked up to him with worship and adoration and when he died [1572.], the lament among the Jews was like on the day of the destruction of the Temple in Jerusalem".

Economic competition between Christian and Jewish merchants resulted in municipal attempts to obtain the *de non tolerandis Judaeis* privilege, which forbade Jews from settling in towns, in which about 20 towns succeeded. In the 16th century the position of the Kazimierz Jews was so strong that in 1564 they were granted a *de non tolerandis christianis* privilege, which prevented non-Jews from acquiring residential or business premises in the Jewish town.

This century and a half was definitely the best period in the history of both of the Jewish and Christian Kazimierz. Such cultural and economic achievement it has never experienced again.

DECLINE AND FALL OF THE TOWN IN THE 17TH AND 18TH CENTURIES

It all started with the capital being transferred to Warsaw in 1609, which dramatically changed the political and economic situation of Kraków and Kazimierz – they became an unimportant province, enlivened only by royal coronations or funerals. The Jews associated with the royal court no longer had access to the king, since – as Bałaban reports – "Warsaw had enjoyed the privilege *de non tolerandis Judaeis* for centuries, and the Warsaw burghers did their best to keep Jews away from the city".

The decline of the prosperous growth of the Jewish community began with fires, which in 1623 and 1643 consumed the vast majority of Jewish buildings. Kazimierz had been afflicted by great fires before (1504, 1557, 1566); however, the conflagration of 1643 marked the beginning of a run of bad luck.

In 1651 the town was afflicted with a terrible plague. Two Kazimierz chroniclers, Marcin Goliński and Stefan Ranotowicz, probably relying on the same source, stated that the death toll "reached 33,638: in Kraków 24-26,000, in Kazimierz 2,578, … 3,500 Jews died.

Four years later Kazimierz suffered the Swedish invasion and occupation of 1655-57, which brought Kazimierz to complete ruin. The Kazimierz townspeople were forced to donate huge monetary contributions to prevent the town from being plundered. The town was still plundered, however, and in 1656 faced famine.

The majority of the town's buildings had been demolished, the town population was halved, the cloth hall, bridges and sewage system ceased to function. The Jewish community was accused of collaborating with the Swedes, which awakened repugnance in their neighbours and led to the escalation of anti-Jewish riots (1660, 1663 and 1682).

In 1670 a flood destroyed the city walls near the Skawińska Gate. The river bed of the Old Vistula silted up in 1675, and from then on the river flowed along the Zakazimierka channel.

During the Great Northern War the Swedish army invaded Kazimierz a number of times between 1702 and 1709. In 1707 another plague took a heavy toll.

Historical disturbances did not spare Kazimierz. The Kazimierz burghers were forced to donate huge monetary contributions, stationed Polish, Russian and Saxon armies, as well as foreign

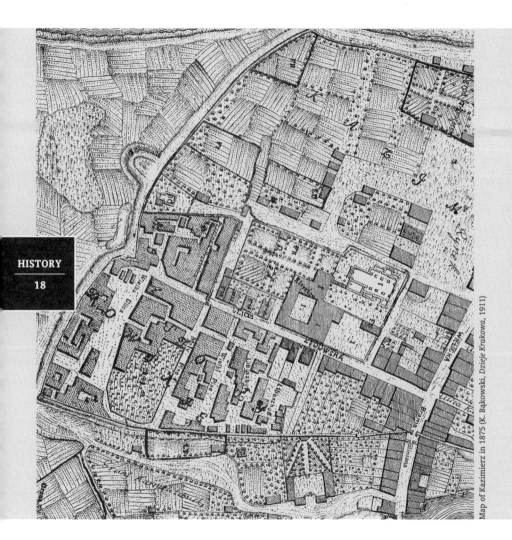

Map of Kazimierz in 1875 (K. Bąkowski, *Dzieje Krakowa*, 1911)

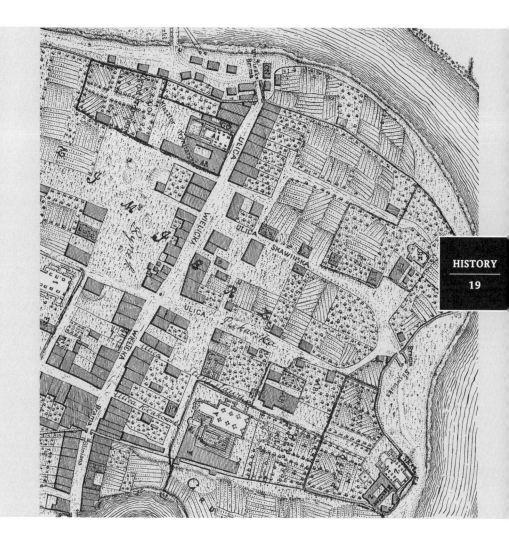

troops marching through Poland, especially during the Seven Years' War (1765-73), caused widespread devastation.

Once pulsating with life, it had become a desolate town. The Christian population fell below 2,000. After the Swedish invasion, the Jewish population numbered 1,800, which meant that it had fallen by two-thirds. Many of those who had fled the town before the invasion never returned. Immigration to Kraków stopped and the exodus to Warsaw followed, for after the invasion it became a political centre.

The town of Kazimierz tried to recover from the fall. However, despite a slight economic improvement and trade growth, the attempt failed. In 1722 Jews came into conflict with the Kraków Commerce Association, as a result of which in 1744 King Augustus III ratified a decree enforcing prohibitions against Jewish commerce in Kraków – Jewish shops had to be closed down and they no longer could trade in cloth, silk and steel. The fact that after the erection of the Isaac Synagogue in 1644 no synagogue was built in Kazimierz for the next 200 years is proof of the critical financial situation of the Kazimierz Jewry.

Intense rebuilding activity took place only in monasteries. The Trinitarian Monastery (Order of the Most Holy Trinity) was erected in ul. Krakowska (1688-95), next to which in the middle of the 18th century the Baroque Church of the Most Holy Trinity, designed by Francisco Placidi, was raised, and on Skałka the late Baroque Church of St Michael the Archangel and St Stanislaus the Bishop Martyr.

Nothing was to save Kazimierz from its final fall. In the troubled time of the Confederation of Bar [Polish civil war against the king and Russia] between 1768-1772, Kazimierz was captured by the Russian army, which used it as an operational base against Kraków. During the four years it passed alternately into the hands of the Russian and Polish armies, causing the town to be, once again, completely devastated. The Kazimierz Jewry, who took a neutral attitude, were ultimately wronged by both sides, which imposed high fines on them.

After the First Partition of 1772 [at the end of the 18th century the partition of Poland (1772, 1793 and 1795) between Russia, Prussia and Austria put an end to Poland's independence for 123 years] Kazimierz was captured by the Austrians – while Kraków remained within Poland – and occupied till 1776, when it returned to Poland in terrible condition. The gates and city walls were still there, although very dilapidated.

In 1776 Jewish commerce in Kraków was again prohibited – therefore over a hundred Jewish traders moved to Kazimierz, which then numbered about 3,500 Jews, to the vicinity of ul. Krakowska where they had to start anew. They renovated the houses and plied their entire trade in Kazimierz. Only second-hand clothes sellers and moneylenders were allowed to remain in Kraków.

In 1796, a year after Poland lost its independence, the Austrian authorities annexed Kazimierz to Kraków, and dissolved the Kazimierz municipality, which was officially confirmed with the decree of 1800.

The year 1800 – the date of the formal annexation of Kazimierz – marks the quietus of Kazimierz as a separate town, which at its beginnings had great aspirations to become the main monarchic centre, university town and a flourishing trade centre. The separate Jewish community in Kazimierz also ceased to exist – all institutions henceforth came under the Kraków municipality. Since then the history of Kazimierz has been inseparably connected with the history of Kraków.

THE 19TH CENTURY – A TIME OF CHANGE

The Austrian authorities (1796-1808) introduced urban renewal to Kazimierz: new streets were laid out, especially in the Jewish town; a permanent bridge across the Vistula was built; wooden buildings were prohibited, church graveyards were liquidated, the Remuh Cemetery was closed down and a new Jewish cemetery established. Finally, streets were cobbled.

In 1801-02 the Austrian authorities ordered the removal of Jews from Kraków proper. As a result, more than 300 pubs, stalls and shops disappeared from Kraków, and by 1804 the Jewish population of Kazimierz had grown to 4,300 (ca. 18% of the Kraków population).

Again Kraków and Kazimierz were occupied by Russian troops, and the disastrous flood of 1813 caused the Kazimierz townspeople to suffer great losses. Established by the Congress of Vienna, the Republic of Kraków (1815-46) meant new legal regulations. The free, independent and strictly neutral city of Kraków and the territory surrounding it was placed under the joint protection of Austria, Prussia and Russia. The city itself had no separate municipal authorities. In 1815 Kraków had a population of 23,400, including 5,000 Jews (21%). *Heders*, religious schools, were closed down, and Jewish children were given general access to public schools.

In 1810 a state school solely for Jewish children was opened, as of 1835 located in the former Kazimierz town hall, whose graduates gave rise to a modern community of assimilated Jews.

As of 1812 Jews were permitted to reside outside the Jewish town, provided that they were assimilated in dress and sent their children to public schools. In the 1840s there were about 200 assimilated Jews. Departing from the Jewish quarter was considered a crime, for which the rabbi would excommunicate. This, however, did not prevent further emigration from the Jewish town.

In the middle of the 19ᵗʰ century serious urban transformations were implemented in Kazimierz. By 1818 the mediaeval city walls of Kazimierz and all gates had been demolished, with a few exceptions (at ul. Paulińska, Podgórska, Miodowa and Szeroka). The vast Kazimierz market had been reduced to present-day Wolnica Square.

Most importantly, the Jewish town renewal took place, which from then on was practically united with Kazimierz. As of 1818 Jews were permitted to reside in all parts of Kazimierz. In 1822 the walls surrounding the Jewish town were demolished. At that time modest neoclassical buildings, the first tenement houses and suburban mansions were erected.

Kraków's location at the point of contact of the three partitioned parts of Poland had a beneficial impact on trade and crafts growth (industry had not developed much). Kraków became a duty-free city, which stimulated trade exchange with Prussia, Austria and Russia. The most profitable professions included grain trade and money-lending – several Jews made large fortunes in financial enterprises in Kraków. Gradually, Jews' contributions to the economic sector in Kraków grew and they gained a monopoly in certain trades and crafts, such as textiles, zinc and shoe-making, and were very active as book-sellers.

A 19ᵗʰ-century mansion in Kazimierz

Hasidism – A religious movement which emerged in the second half of the 18th century as a result of the spiritual and physical trauma the Jews in eastern Poland and the present Ukraine were undergoing after the Chmielnicki massacres. The chief leader of the movement was the charismatic Ba'al Shem Tov, (Israel ben Eliezer; 1700-60). The movement combined *Kabala* with popular traditions of ecstasy and mass enthusiasm. It soon became extremely popular among the masses and was the subject of attacks by the Reform circles. In the course of time the movement lost its protest character and became an institutionalised form of Orthodoxy, opposing modernity in Judaism.

Haskala – A Hebrew term for the Enlightenment movement and ideology which began within the Jewish society of the 1770s, with the originator Moses Mendelssohn (1729-86), a philosopher known as the "Jewish Socrates", and the translator of the Hebrew Bible into German. The Haskala followers, known as *Maskilim*, aimed to assimilate in language, dress and manners, to secularise their education and so on. They were subject to Orthodox attacks. In Kraków, the *Maskilim* propagated pro-Polish tendencies aimed at 'cultural assimilation', not religious. The most famous Haskala supporters include: Jonatan Warszauer (1820-1888), a doctor and philanthropist, and Józef Oettinger (1818-1895), a doctor, a graduate and the first Jewish lecturer at the Jagiellonian University.

Kraków became a lively intellectual and political centre for Polish patriots, and more and more Jews became involved in the independence movement. Dow Ber Meisels, a Kraków rabbi who was actively engaged in revolutionary activities, was able to combine an attachment to Jewish tradition with a sense of Polish patriotism (see box, p. 69).

In the first half of the 19th century two antagonistic movements opposed by the Orthodox society spread to Kazimierz: *Hasidism*, a pietistic religious movement that began in the 18th century, and *Haskala*, the Jewish Enlightenment, an intellectual movement among the Jewish intelligentsia and bourgeoisie. Both movements' members established their own prayer houses – in 1815 the first Hasidic prayer house was established.

In the 1840s the Reform Jews, or *Maskilim*, intellectuals, members of the Haskala, settled in Kazimierz and were immediately attacked by the antagonistic Hasidic and Orthodox communities. In 1862 the newcomers erected the Reform Synagogue, called Tempel, which became the centre of assimilation supporters.

Despite obstinate opposition, members of all three communities had one common aim: the struggle for the social emancipation of the Jews. However, only after the internal reforms within the Austrian Empire were social transformations possible. In 1867 Jews were granted equal citizenship rights. Locally, this meant the long-desired opportunity to reside in Kraków, from which they had been expelled in 1495.

A Kraków saint, Adam Chmielowski, also known as Brother Albert, concerned about the poverty in Kazimierz, after 1892 established a number of shelter houses for the poor and homeless.

The Jewish community erected (1854-66) at their own expense a Jewish hospital in ul. Skawińska, which could boast the most distinguished physicians, the most modern medical equipment and the highest standard of care. In 1899 the first public Judaic Library, *Ezra*, was founded.

As the Habsburg monarchy transformed itself into the Austro-Hungarian Empire, Galicia (the southern part of Poland) obtained local autonomy (1866-1918) and Kazimierz changed entirely – multi-storey tenement houses and sumptuous buildings were raised. Another hospital was erected by the Brothers Hospitallers between 1897-1906 in ul. Trynitarska. The Old Vistula riverbed was covered up (1873) and a park was established there (now ul. Józefa Dietla), which was considered the greatest public achievement of the time.

Thanks to the gasworks established in Kazimierz, the first gas lamps were illuminated in 1857 in the Main Market Square in Kraków. The first horse-drawn omnibus ran from the Podgórski Bridge to the Railway Station in 1867, and in 1882 was replaced by narrow-gauge horse trams. A tram depot was built here between 1882-1888, and in 1905 the first municipal power station.

KAZIMIERZ BECOMES THE JEWISH QUARTER

Toward the end of the 19th century Kazimierz was almost exclusively inhabited by Jews. The Jewish population had grown from 13,500 in 1850 (33% of the entire population) to 32,000 in 1910 (22% of the population, due to the city of Kraków's expansion). Poorer Jews resided in the former Jewish town, unable to part with the synagogues and the atmosphere. The better-off moved to other suburbs, such as Podgórze, where another Jewish community existed (till 1937).

Orthodox Jews speaking Yiddish, who were barely integrated with the Christian society, were the vast majority. They earned their livelihood trading with Christians, and scrupulously followed the Talmud and their rabbi. The conservative and Reform communities also had their rabbis, but their members were much more integrated with the Christian

Adam Chmielowski (1845-1916), a painter. One day he experienced a mystic vision and became aware of the human misery of the poor, which brought on his spiritual metamorphosis. This well-known artist, involved in the cultural and artistic life of Kraków, abandoned painting and at the age of 42 turned to help those in need – the homeless. In 1887 he took the name of Brother Albert and founded the Brothers of the Third Order of Saint Francis, Servants of the Poor, also known as the Albertines, to ensure the continuity of this initiative. Then, in 1891, he founded the women's congregation of the Order. Adam Chmielowski was canonised in 1989 by Pope John Paul II.

society. They spoke Polish, stood for municipal elections – in 1905 Józef Sare was the first Jew to be elected deputy mayor of Kraków; they were members of the legal, medical and teaching professions (e.g. professors at the Jagiellonian University), as well as of municipal administration. At the turn of the 19th and 20th centuries Kazimierz resounded with three languages: Yiddish (Orthodox Jews), Hebrew (Zionists) and Polish (Reform assimilation supporters).

The second half of the 19th century witnessed the rise of Jewish political parties aiming at the propagation of Zionist ideas, calling for a return of the Jewish people to Israel and for a Hebrew revival. The Committee of the Delegates of the Zionist Organisations of Western Galicia was established in Kraków and presided over by Osias Thon, a rabbi of the liberal Kraków congregation for almost 30 years, an excellent preacher who was elected to the first Polish Parliament in 1919. The Zionist-Socialist movement *Po'alei Zion* was founded in Kraków, as well as a faction of the world-wide religious Zionist movement, *Mizrachi*.

In the interwar period large political parties were formed, such as *Agudat Israel* which sought to preserve Orthodoxy; *Hitahadut*, the Socialist-Zionist labour party, representing secular Jewish society; and the General Jewish Workers' Union Bund, the Jewish labour movement.

Many Jews became prominent in the cultural and social life of Kraków, among them professors of philology, historians, scholars, painters, jurists and doctors. The growth of education took place – the largest religious school, *Talmud Torah*, enrolled 1,500 pupils; in the interwar period a modern religious secondary school, *Heder*, was founded; and in 1917 Sara Shnirer founded the Beis Yakov Girls' School for Orthodox girls, whose fame has lasted till the present day. Jewish youth studied at the Academy of Fine Arts and the Jagiellonian University. Between 1866 and 1918 1,462 Jews studied in the law and medicine faculties of the Jagiellonian University, and in 1923-24 Jewish students constituted 32% of the total student population (in subsequent years the *numerus clausus* was introduced and the percentage fell to 12%). The B'nei B'rith Association built a Jewish Hall of Residence at ul. Przemyska 3.

Among prominent Kraków artists were the famous Jewish painter Maurycy Gottlieb (1856-79), Jan Matejko's student at the Kraków School of Fine Arts, a representative of realism and romanticism, whose major work *Jews Praying on the Day of Atonement* is considered a masterpiece, and the painter Abraham Neumann (1873-1942). In 1908 the first theatre was founded on the corner of ul. Gazowa and Bocheńska, where various troupes performed. In 1926 the Jonas Turkov Theatre arrived in Kraków and he himself was entrusted with the Kraków Jewish Theatre, where Yiddish adaptations of the works of world and Jewish literature were shown and where the magnificent Ida Kamińska performed.

Also deeply bound with Kraków and Kazimierz was the outstanding Jewish poet Mordechai Gebirtig (1877-1942), the author of the afore-mentioned poem *Farewell, my Kraków* (see Introduction).

Religious life flourished – in the interwar period Kraków could boast 8 community synagogues and about 80 prayer houses located all over the city. Still, the heart of Judaism lay in ul. Szeroka with its 4 synagogues, 4 prayer houses, a mikvah, a ritual bath house, and the Remuh Cemetery.

During World War I the town was endangered by military operations, but was not destroyed thanks to the Austrian fortifications. However, the upheavals of the war, widespread unemployment, and famine throughout the city intensified anti-Semitism.

In the interwar period the Jewish population grew from 45,200 in 1921 to 56,600 (25.8% of the total) in 1931. In the late 1930s the Jewish population numbered 60,000 and was the fourth biggest Jewish community in Poland. About 45% of Kraków Jews were occupied in commerce and insurance, 35% in crafts, and the position of the medical and legal professions had grown stronger.

The Jewish press also flourished then – about 66 newspapers and periodicals were published in Kraków: 34 in Polish, 24 in Yiddish, the remainder in Hebrew. The most crucial was the Zionist daily *Nowy Dziennik*, which had considerable public influence.

Zionist political activity intensified; Jews were permanently represented by the local authorities, and customarily one of the deputy mayors of Kraków was Jewish. Jewish social life thrived all over Kraków in the theatres, cinemas and cafés.

Throughout the 19th and the beginning of the 20th centuries Kazimierz had changed its status entirely – it ceased to be a separate town and became one of Kraków's suburbs, it recovered from urban decline, began prospering economically, and also had become exclusively the Jewish quarter, described in the 1930s by the often-quoted Majer Bałaban: "Today Jews reside in Kraków and all its outskirts; the Orthodox remain in Kazimierz, and in the 'Jewish town' only the poor and ultra-conservative, who cannot part with those old streets and synagogues. Amid the neighbouring modern streets with tall buildings the 'Jewish town' looks like a forgotten island that has been dozing for centuries. Only on market days does Szeroka Street fill up with the poor of the great city, seeking buyers for old linen or worn-out clothes. Also on Saturdays and Jewish festivals the town is crowded with people; endless processions of Jews in silk capotes [coats], and fur-trimmed hats wander to synagogues and *battei-ha-midrash* [prayer houses], the greatest crowd gathering here on the day of the minor festival *Lag ba-Omer*. On that day thousands, perhaps hundreds of thousands, of religious Jews from all over the Polish Republic come to Kraków's Kazimierz to pray at the grave of the great Remuh (Rabbi Moses Isserles), whose anniversary of death falls on that minor festival".

Kazimierz remained the Jewish quarter until the outbreak of World War II, charged with a unique atmosphere, specific culture and unparalleled local colour.

Today this world no more exists – the world portrayed by Szymon Dankowicz, a preacher of the Reform Synagogue, at the ceremony of the second funeral of King Casimir the Great in 1869, as "Polish Jerusalem". World War II put an end to the flourishing Jewish community, when almost the entire Jewish population was murdered, and the fascinating world that had been present in Kazimierz for almost 450 years and in Kraków, almost 700 ceased to exist.

THE HOLOCAUST

At the outbreak of World War II the Jewish population in Poland numbered 3.5 million, which constituted 10% of the total population. In Kraków and its vicinity, according to the 1939 census conducted by the Jewish community in November, by German order, there were 68,482 Jews, in Kraków proper about 60,000 (25% of the total population).

Soon after the German occupation of Kraków (on 6th September, 1939) implementation of the policy towards Jews began. It aimed at the gradual restriction of their rights, the plunder of their property, deprivation of the material basis of their existence, isolation from the non-

Jewish society of Kraków, physical extermination through slave labour and deportations to concentration and death camps.

German authorities began to issue regulations aimed at the discrimination and humiliation of Jewish citizens of Kraków. "Lawlessness was visible from the early days of the war" – recalls Aleksander Bieberstein, doctor and head of the isolation hospital in the ghetto, and author of *Annihilation of Jews in Kraków* – "We witnessed assaults, raids, batteries, cutting off of the beards of Orthodox Jews, robbing pedestrians of their jewellery, robbing flats of furniture, robbing wares from shops. Soon apprehensions followed – in the early days the Zucker family from Stradom St. and the Schickmanns from Grodzka St. were apprehended and none of them returned".

From 8th September, 1939 all Jewish shops, cafés, restaurants and companies had to be marked with the Star of David in a visible place, which facilitated German raids; on 20th November, 1939 all bank accounts were frozen, and Jewish companies and workshops were confiscated; from 23th November, 1939 all Jews had to wear a white armband with the Star of David (10 cm wide with a star 8 cm in diameter) under threat of the death penalty (as of 1940). Compulsory labour was imposed (on Saturdays and Jewish festivals), kosher slaughter was prohibited, all synagogues and prayer houses were closed down (26th Oct., 1939). All vehicles were confiscated, there were separate tram compartments for Jews and non-Jews, and Jews were not permitted to enter public places such as the Main Market Square, and non-Jewish theatres, cafés and restaurants.

23 members of the Jewish community were appointed to the Jewish Council (*Judenrat*) that faced the extremely difficult task of administering German regulations. The first two presidents of the congregation, Prof. Marek Bieberstein and Dr Artur Rosenzweig, and members of the first board – according to Aleksander Bieberstein – "were people of high moral standards, with an extremely social attitude to work, putting the Jewish community's welfare and its protection against German persecution first. They showed selfless devotion to work, often risking their health and lives. … The subsequent board [after Artur Rosenzweig's execution in June 1942], presided over by David Gutter and Dr Samuel Streimer, was entirely at the invaders' service, especially the Gestapo. They followed all German instructions pedantically, often with great eagerness, suggesting their own ideas for robbing and maltreating the Jewish society".

The Jewish Police (*Ordnungsdienst*, 'Service for Keeping Order'– OD), established in August 1940, was to administer order in the ghetto regime, assist the Germans in apprehensions, deportations to death camps, and hunting for conspirators and Jews hiding on the Aryan side. Those lacking high moral standards often eagerly obeyed the Nazi Germans, hoping to survive, although these were false hopes since most of the so-called 'OD-men' were executed.

On 6th November, 1939, 183 professors (including several Jews) of the Jagiellonian University and other Kraków universities were insidiously arrested and shipped to concentration camps in Dachau and Sachsenhausen.

All private Jewish schools were closed down (11th Dec., 1939), and Jewish students and teachers expelled from state schools. At the outbreak of WW II there were 6 Jewish elementary schools (2,100 pupils), 3 private secondary and vocational schools (2,800 pupils), and about 1,500 pupils were enrolled in non-Jewish state schools.

In April 1940 compulsory labour was imposed on all Jews between 12-60 years of age and from then on Jews were exploited as a cheap workforce. Initially, the slave labourers had to remove rubble, shovel snow, and later on work in factories and workshops in the ghettos and camps.

Since Kraków was the capital of German-occupied Poland, the governor-general of Poland, Hans Frank, ordered in April 1940 that the city should become *Judefrei*, 'clean of Jews', and issued an order of mass evacuation of Jews from Kraków. Between mid-1940 and the beginning of 1941 about 40,000-60,000 Jews left, while about 15,000 received special permission to remain and many arrived here from neighbouring communities seeking refuge in Kraków. The deportees were transferred to the Lublin area and between 1942 and 1943 died in death camps at Bełżec, Sobibor and Treblinka.

TIME OF PARTINGS
– THE KRAKÓW GHETTO 1941-43

On 3rd March, 1941 an order was issued to establish a Jewish residence district in Podgórze (the term ghetto was not used). Jews had to move there by 20th March, 1941. The non-Jewish residents of Podgórze were allocated ex-Jewish homes in Kazimierz. The mass removal began. As Aleksander Bieberstein recalls: "Jewish property was transferred to the new residences by various means of transport. … Because of the time pressure, migrating lasted all day long, from early morning to late evening, accompanied by noise, lamenting and complaints. The image of Kazimierz changed. The character of that Kraków quarter, for centuries inhabited by Jews, faded away. Families bound with Kazimierz for generations left, restaurants and synagogues were closed down".

On 21th March, 1941 the ghetto was closed, enclosed by a 3-metre wall, with a semi-circular top resembling Jewish tombstones. More than

16,000 people were crowded in 320 houses, which, prior to the ghetto establishment, had been inhabited by 3,000 people. From 15th October, 1941, departing from the ghetto was punishable by death.

Lack of space (often rooms were shared by 2-4 families), fear, and a feeling of insecurity turned everyday life into a nightmare. In October 1941 Jews from the neighbouring communities were transferred to the Kraków ghetto, whose population had grown by 6,000.

The ghetto comprised the Jewish Council office, 3 Jewish hospitals, the labour department (*Arbeitsamt*), orphanage, old people's home, Jewish Social Self-Help association, bath houses, handicraft workshops, German and Jewish police stations, prison, and the union workshops for Jewish craftsmen working for *Zentrale für Handwerkslieferungen* situated in the former Optima chocolate factory, the Julius Madritsch garment factory, the Feliks Dziuba Optical Glass-works, and, outside the ghetto, the Oskar Schindler Enamelware Factory.

Also situated inside the ghetto was the Pharmacy 'Under the Eagle', whose owner Tadeusz Pankiewicz (see p. 99), the only non-Jewish person allowed to reside in the ghetto, wrote a stirring memoir called *The Cracow Ghetto Pharmacy*.

The first deportations took place between 1st-8th June, 1942. Those who had not received permis-

Symche Spira, the head of Jewish police (OD), a glazier by profession and until the war, full-bearded and wearing a long black capote – suddenly became a 'big shot'. ... This man, blindly dedicated to the Germans, carried out with utmost precision every German order (...). He would guess and anticipate their thinking, (...) and impress them with his unquestioning zeal. Their commands were important to him, nothing else mattered. Symche Spira was a megalomaniac, wrapped in fantasy, a classic example of a psychopath, neurotic, ... a human machine, an unthinking robot, carrying out the Gestapo orders as if hypnotised.

T. Pankiewicz, *The Cracow Ghetto Pharmacy*
[All quotations from T. Pankiewicz, *The Cracow Ghetto Pharmacy*, by courtesy of Professor Simcha Ronen of Tel Aviv University]

sion to stay in the ghetto had to gather at Zgody Square (now Bohaterów Getta Square), as well as at the courtyard of the Optima factory, and then walk to the railway station in Płaszów. About 7,000 victims were deported to the Bełżec death camp and several hundred were put to death in the ghetto itself, especially on 4th June, 'Bloody Thursday', when the 60-year-old poet Mordechai Gebirtig, together with his family, and the painter Abraham Neumann were shot.

Another *Aktion*, deportation, took place on 28th October, 1942. According to Bieberstein, "All previous deportations were bloody and brutal, but the 1942 October action with its barbarity, bestiality and cruelty exceeded all that Jews in the Kraków ghetto had experienced before. This time the patients at hospitals were included in the deportation. About 4,500 Jews were shipped to Bełżec, while the chronically ill, the old people's home inmates and the 300 children at the orphanage were murdered on the spot".

As a result of the deportations many people committed suicide, and carrying a lethal dose of cyanide was very common. The area of the ghetto had diminished in size, and in December 1942 was divided into two parts: A – for the employed, B – for the unemployed. Initially, they were both easily accessible, but in the course of time it became impossible to move from part B to part A. The German authorities established *Kinderheim*, the Children's Home, for orphaned children under 14, as well as day-care centre for children whose parents worked. Mothers were separated from their children extremely reluctantly, bearing in mind the October deportations.

All the above regulations were preparation for the dramatic ending, which took place on 13th and 14th March, 1943, when the Kraków ghetto was liquidated. All the Part A inhabitants were transferred to the nearby camp in Płaszów. Children under 14 had to remain in the ghetto *Kinderheim*, and, as officially assured, they would be transferred to Płaszów the following day.

Oskar Schindler (1908-74), was born in Zittau, near Brünnlitz in Moravia. In the 1930s he joined the Nazi Party (Nationalist Socialist German Workers' Party).

Soon after the outbreak of World War II, as a Nazi member of the German intelligence (*Abwehr*) he arrived in Kraków, where he resided at ul. Straszewskiego 7, at the foot of Wawel Hill (which also served as Schindler's house in the film *Schindler's List*). He soon won over the key officers in the SS (Nazi elite) and the German army (*Wehrmacht*) by his unusual personal charm, and by his seemingly inexhaustible supply of desired goods acquired from the black market, such as cognac, cigars, coffee and beautiful ladies, which involved him in activity not necessarily compliant with Nazi policy.

In order to avoid being sent to the front, he bought a bankrupt enamelware factory from its Jewish owner, Abraham Bankier, in December 1939. Soon the *Deutsche Emalien Fabrik*, or 'Emalia', using Jewish labour, commenced the production of enamelware for the German army. Schindler's key contact with the Jewish world was Icchak Stern (played by Ben Kingsley in the film), the accountant for the very profitable factory. After the establishment of the ghetto, the Jews were escorted to the factory by the police. In 1943, thanks to his numerous connections and bribes, Schindler managed to obtain permission to establish a Płaszów sub-camp on the territory of the factory. He built barracks there and provided Jews working for him with relative peace. They were not exposed to everyday torture, exhausting roll-calls, lashing and death (Bieberstein).

As the Eastern Front closed in, the Nazis liquidated camps, and in the summer of 1944 the inmates of the sub-camp at Schindler's factory were sent to Płaszów. Schindler then established a weapons factory and a sub-camp in Brünnlitz, where Emalia's former workers were to be hired. It was then that the famous list of people to be transferred to Brünnlitz was made. A number of myths and legends exist concerning the creation of the list. Nevertheless, Marcel Goldberg, a Jewish policeman, undoubtedly had a large part to play in its establishment; he took bribes in exchange for including people on the list. Finally, the list comprised the names of about 1,100 Jewish workers. In October 1944 they were transferred to Brünnlitz, but 300 women were mistakenly shipped to the Auschwitz-Birkenau death camp. Schindler managed to rescue the women, and after a month they were sent to Brünnlitz.

The munitions produced at the factory are said to have been faulty, and ultimately Schindler bought munitions elsewhere and sold them as his own manufacture. Schindler and his wife Emilie procured food and medicine for the Brünnlitz inmates. In 1945 prisoners evacuated from other German camps joined the Brünnlitz camp. On 6th May, 1945 the German officers abandoned the camp, and the Jews, known as *Schindlerjuden*, bid regretful farewell to Schindler that night. The Russian army liberated the camp on 9th May, 1945.

Schindler's post-war life was characterised by a lack of achievement – both in business, and in married life. He emigrated to Argentina, went bankrupt there, abandoned his wife and returned to Germany in 1958. He was provided financially by the *Schindlerjuden* and the Jewish Association B'nei B'rith.

In 1962 he was recognised as one of the 'Righteous Among the Nations' and awarded a medal with the Talmud inscription: "Whoever saves one life, saves the world entire". A tree was planted in honour of him in the 'Avenue of the Righteous Among the Nations'. He died in 1974 in Frankfurt, and, according to his wish, was buried in the Catholic cemetery in Israel.

On 14th March, 1943 over 1,000 Part B inhabitants (the elderly, ill, unemployed, children and their mothers who had decided to remain in the ghetto) were executed in Zgody Square and neighbouring streets. All surviving hospital patients together with several doctors were shot. About 2,000 people were deported to the Auschwitz death camp and over 6,000 people transferred to the Płaszów camp. Afterwards, SS-men searched the deserted ghetto and all found hiding in the flats, attics or cellars were shot.

In the final days of the ghetto many people managed to escape through the sewage system and survive with the help of Poles. One of such refugees was Prof. Julian Aleksandrowicz, who survived together with his wife and son. He was a prominent figure, a 'Cracovian of the 20th Century' and the author of the memoirs *Kartki z dziennika doktora Twardego* [Pages of Doctor Twardy's Diary].

THE PŁASZÓW CAMP

Established in the autumn of 1942 on the territory of two Jewish cemeteries (10 hectares), this was initially a work camp. It was expanded rapidly toward the end of 1942 by German, Polish and Jewish workers. Amon Goeth attempted to erect the industrial and crafts barracks that would work for the army as fast as possible, for only such production would protect its administration from being sent to the front (Bieberstein). In March 1943 6,000 ghetto inhabitants were transferred here. Amon Goeth had been the commander of the camp since February 1943, and his reign meant total lawlessness towards the camp prisoners – he would punish each 'offence', even the pettiest, by death, and he would either shoot the victims he had chosen himself, or give an order to shoot or hang someone. In January 1944 Płaszów became a concentration camp. According to initial plans, the camp was meant for 2-4,000, but in fact the prison population numbered 25,000, and its area reached 80 hectares in the middle of 1944. Apart from fenced residential German, Polish and Jewish barracks (men and women separately), the camp comprised numerous industrial barracks, where tailor, furrier, upholstery, electric, watch-making, locksmith, sheet metal, shoe-making, brush-making, and the Madritsch garment workshops were located.

Mass executions were conducted at two undulations (the former Austrian fortifications and WWI artillery units) – at 'Hujowa Hill' (named after Albert Hujar, a particularly cruel SS-man [in Polish an offensive word meaning male sexual organ]) and at 'Lipowy Pit'. The Montelupi prisoners, mainly Poles but also denounced Jewish conspirators, possessing 'Aryan papers', and Jewish prisoners sentenced to death, as well as the elderly, ill or 'selected' were executed here. Most of them never entered the camp registration, but the estimates are that about 8,000 people were murdered here. In August 1944 the camp prisoners had to exhume the dead bodies and burn them, in order to dispose of the evidence of the crime.

In a separate camp, about 2,000 Polish and Roma (Gypsy) inmates were held prisoner. Their population grew dramatically after the outbreak of the Warsaw Uprising in August 1944, when 6,000 Poles were arrested and imprisoned in the Płaszów camp.

As the Red Army drew closer, concentration camps were liquidated and prisoners transferred westward or murdered. Therefore, the camp migration increased, particularly in 1944, when many people were brought here from smaller camps in eastern Małopolska, as well as Slovakia and Hungary, and then shipped from Płaszów to death camps in Auschwitz and Germany (Flossenbürg, Mauthausen, Gross-Rosen, Brünnlitz). At a rough estimate about 25,000 prisoners passed through the camp. In January 1945, just before the Russian Army entered Kraków, the remaining 550 men and 150 women were marched from the camp. Ashes of the Jews, Poles and Gypsies put to death by slave labour and executions rest on the territory of the Płaszów camp.

Amon Goeth was arrested in September 1944 under a German court order due to theft of Jewish possessions and financial fraud, and immediately after the war he was brought to trial for crimes against humanity and sentenced to death by the Supreme Tribunal in Kraków. He was hanged in Kraków on 13th September, 1946.

The Kraków Jews began organising an active resistance movement at the end of 1940. It mainly consisted of youth organisations: *Akiva*, headed by Adolf Libeskind and Szymon Dränger, *Dror-Frajhajt* headed by Abraham Lejbowicz, and *Haszomer Hacair* led by Hersz Bauminger and Bernard Halbreich, which later merged into the countrywide ŻOB ('Jewish Fighting Organisation'). Their members were involved in sabotage and armed resistance (derailment of trains, the murder of a German officer), but their activity never developed on a larger scale, and there was no armed uprising as in Warsaw. An attack of great significance took place on 22nd (or 24th according to some sources) December, 1942, when the Kraków ŻOB group planted a bomb at the Kraków Cyganeria Club; in consequence several German officers died and several were injured. Unfortunately, the majority of the resistance group were arrested soon afterwards.

Many mothers distrusted the Germans, did not have faith in their assurances; they were not willing to leave their children alone. They therefore left the ranks of their group and went over to Ghetto B, whose existence is calculated to last another 24 hours. Most of all the men remained in the ranks, surrendering to the persuasion of their wives; they deceived themselves into believing that they would be able to do something for their dear ones; they expected a miracle. (...) Unforgettable impressions of those poignant scenes were indelibly etched in the minds of all who witnessed them. Total strangers cried, observing the pain of those who remained in utter helplessness. This was a thousand times more horrible than physical torture and murder of the defenseless.

T. Pankiewicz, *The Cracow Ghetto Pharmacy*

Until the present day the question of why the Jews did not defend themselves has been raised. A good answer has been provided by Tadeusz Pankiewicz, eye-witness of those times: "Anyone who did not see at first hand the awesome horror could not understand or grasp the dire circumstances that plagued these people. They could not fathom the perfidious lies which misled them the day before their death. If my questioners could spend even a few hours in the funereal atmosphere in which these *Aktions* took place ... At every few steps someone was killed, beaten, hu-miliated and tortured. ... If one could see the perpetrators, observe the means they used to instill fear and terror, cruelly shooting, and then deceiving the 'resettled' with a hope that they would live; if the inquirers knew about the threats of revenge on the entire family for even thinking about escape, for sabotage and for any self-defence action – he would no longer ask 'why'. ... I did not hear any pleading, whining or crying. People faced death calmly, resignedly and proudly. The Germans did not see their terrorised victims whimpering and sobbing for mercy".

The Jewish Social Self-Help association delivered aid to Jews in that dire situation from the early days of the war, providing them with food, medicine, foreign donations and supervising aid committees. As of March 1943 the Żegota Council for Aiding the Jews supported numerous Jews with shelter and care outside the ghetto, forged documents, transfers abroad, and appeals and mobilisation of the Polish Underground and the entire society, although for many Jews help came too late. Also, individual people provided help by smuggling needed products to the ghetto (e.g. throwing them out of a tram, through less-guarded gates or at workshops and factories outside the ghetto), storing or cashing valuable objects, obtaining fake identification papers or hiding Jews on the so-called Aryan side.

A touching poem, *Es brent*, by the afore-mentioned poet Mordechai Gebirtig, became extremely popular among the resistance groups. The poem is likely to have been written in reference to a pogrom in the town of Przytyk in 1936, and then became the hymn of the fighters in the Warsaw ghetto:

It's burning, brothers, it's burning!
Oy, our poor shtetl is burning,
Raging winds are fanning with wild flames
And furiously tearing,
Destroying and scattering everything.
All around, all is burning
And you stand and look just so, you
With folded hands…!
And you stand and look just so,
while our shtetl burns.

It's burning, brothers, it's burning!
Oy, our poor shtetl is burning,
The moment is at hand when, God forbid,
Our town, along with all of us,
Will be turned to ashes by the flames,
And only bare, black walls will remain
As after a battle.

Our town is burning,
And only you can save it!
Extinguish the fire with your very blood,
If you must!

Don't just stand there, brothers,
With folded hands.
Don't stand there, put out the fire!
Our shtetl is burning!
Mordechai Gebirtig (transl. E.G. Mlotek)

Poland was the only German-occupied country where helping the Jews was punishable by death (H. Frank's order of 15th Oct., 1941). It is a formidable task to give a clear-cut statement on the Christian attitude: some delivered aid while risking their own lives; some preferred to turn a blind eye to Jewish persecution, in order to avoid taking action; and some actively participated in the extermination of Jews. There appears a temptation to evaluate these attitudes; this, nevertheless, – from the present perspective – is impossible, for we are unable to comprehend the appalling conditions in which people were then put, and unable to project how we would

Zofia Kossak-Szczucka, who headed 'Żegota', issued a leaflet in which she decried both the Jewish annihilation and the Polish silence: "The world is looking at that atrocity, more outrageous than anything else in its history, and remains silent. The massacre of millions of helpless people is being conducted amidst a general, ominous silence [that] can no longer be tolerated. Whatever its reasons – it is despicable. One cannot be passive in the face of crime. He who remains silent when confronted with manslaughter – becomes an accomplice of the murderers. He who does not condemn – approves".

Quoted from: E. Duda, *The Jews of Cracow*

act under these conditions, especially since action taken depended individually on character and personal courage.

It is estimated that about 3,000 to 5,000 (5-8% of the total) of Kraków Jews survived the Holocaust, including about 1,100 Jews saved by Schindler. Thus came the irreversible twilight of a certain epoch – Jewish Kraków, which had been one of the largest Jewish centres prior to World War II, had disappeared. Cultural, economic and political life had flourished here and prominent rabbis, scholars and artists had lived and worked here. The Holocaust put an end to nearly 700 years of Polish-Jewish history.

KAZIMIERZ AFTER 1945

Only after the Kraków liberation (18th Jan., 1945) did surviving Jews return to Kraków and Kazimierz from Russia where they had been deported, from the vicinity of Kraków where they had found shelter during the war years, or from concentration camps. Yet their former quarter had been entirely changed: Christians resided in their former houses, synagogues and other community buildings had been destroyed or taken over by the municipality, and cemeteries had been devastated. Utterly exhausted, seeking their relatives, in need of housing, food, medical care, and above all support and human sympathy, instead, they faced hatred, which led to a 'blood libel pogrom' on 11th August, 1945. For many this was the last straw, leading them to emigrate, mostly to the United States and Palestine. Establishment of the State of Israel in 1948 caused mass exodus of Jews from Poland. The 1945-50 official censuses reveal large fluctuations in the Jewish population of Kraków: 1945–500, 1947–20,000, 1950–4,000.

Between 1944 and 1949 there were attempts to re-establish the economic, cultural and political life of the Kraków Jews, although it proved next to impossible after 1950. The Jewish Historical Committee examined and documented Hitlerite atrocities in Kraków. The reactivated Jewish Community in Kraków, managed to retrieve 5 synagogues, and finance the renovation of two of them – the Remuh and Tempel.

Successive waves of emigrations in the years 1956-57 and 1968-69 contributed to the dramatic fall in the Jewish population in Poland and Kraków. A handful of Jews remained, mainly the elderly, lonely or ill, scattered across the city.

Since 1949 the former Jewish school in the Kazimierz town hall has hosted the Ethnographical Museum (see Route 2). The Popper Synagogue was turned into the Kazimierz Culture Club in 1965, while the High Synagogue became the Maintenance of the Kraków Monuments Committee Studio in 1972. The rebuilt and fully restored Old Synagogue (1955-59) hosts the Judaica Branch of the Historical Museum of Krakow (its first exhibition was opened in 1961), and in the late 1950s the Remuh Cemetery was renovated.

Kazimierz faced another crisis in the 1960s and 1970s, related to the anti-Semitic policy of the communist authorities. By the late 1960s Jewish shops and workshops had vanished from Kazimierz. Apart from the religious Jewish Community of Kraków, the secular Social and Cultural Association of Jews existed until 1968. Thanks to the efforts of the presidents of the Jewish Community of Kraków, Maciej Jakubowicz and his son Czesław, two synagogues continued to function in Kraków

The last mass emigration was a result of the anti-Semitic campaign of March 1968. The socio-political ferment steadily gathering strength from the late 1950s, combined with the leadership crisis of the Polish Communist Party, culminated in <u>March 1968</u>. The communist authorities relied on the workable remedy of anti-Semitism. During the Arab-Israeli 'Six-Day War' of 1967, the communist authorities declared their support of the Arab countries, and accused Polish Jews of supporting the State of Israel, with which diplomatic relations had been dissolved. In June 1967 Władysław Gomułka, the first secretary of the Central Committee of the Polish United Workers' Party (PZPR) from 1956 to 1970, gave a speech in which he acknowledged the existence of the so-called 'fifth column' of Jews disloyal to the socialist Polish state. His speech encouraged a nationwide 'anti-Zionist' campaign that resulted in purges within the party, administration and army. About 30,000 people of Jewish origin emigrated. Often people who were not Jewish were accused of 'Zionism'. The March Campaign, conducted by the party in collaboration with security forces and the army, led to the ultimate annihilation of Jewish life in Poland.

– the Remuh and Tempel. However, in the 1980s services were conducted without a rabbi, but in the presence of two cantors. Due to the small number of Kraków Jews, the services were held in the Remuh Synagogue only, and in a greatly simplified form, since very few members of the community knew Hebrew. Kazimierz had become the symbol of Jewish absence.

Post-war Kazimierz under communist rule had been left behind. No investment into renovation nor restoration of the old buildings was made, for it was assumed that there was no such need, since Kraków had not been bombed during World War II. Thus, the devastation and decline of post-war Kazimierz turned many historical monuments into ruins, causing them to be demolished, and Kazimierz's historical character was to some extent destroyed.

Christian Kazimierz was kept alive during the yearly procession from Wawel to Skałka on St Stanislaus Day (8th May), the most significant religious festival of national character, especially under the rule of Archbishop Karol Wojtyła, the present Pope.

Life in Kazimierz died away. It became a poor, neglected district, forgotten by all. There were more and more dilapidated ruins among which one dreaded to walk after dusk. Only in 1978

An observant visitor will notice traces of the former Jewish presence

was the Civic Committee for the Renovation of Krakow Monuments founded to finance the restoration of neglected Kazimierz.

NEW LIFE IN KAZIMIERZ

Kazimierz has enjoyed a genuine renaissance since the fall of the communist regime in 1989. A revival of interest in Jewish culture, particularly among young people, has emerged. On the one hand, it has resulted from the need to recover their own identity, especially for people who have just discovered their Jewish roots; on the other hand, it has been associated with the discovery of Jewish traditions and culture by Christian circles, which constitutes a unique phenomenon on a world scale.

In 1988 the very first edition of the Jewish Culture Festival took place. The communists still ruled, therefore the Festival had a rather unofficial character and broke the communist taboo in the People's Republic of Poland concerning Jewish issues, e.g. by the academic session *Jews and Poles – A Cultural Encounter*, by showing, for the first time after the Second World War, films in Yiddish that had been made in Poland, and by a series of concerts, theatre performances and exhibitions that was the first step in recovering and remembering the history and culture of this once Jewish town, which had fallen into oblivion after all those years. The second edition of the Festival was held in 1990 after the victory of Solidarity (*Solidarność*). Since 1994 the Festival has been organised every year and has gained worldwide fame (the 13th edition took place in 2003) and has been attracting the most outstanding Jewish artists, lecturers and other prominent figures, as well as thousands of participants from Poland and all over the world, who have the opportunity to meet and take delight in Jewish culture in various fields of art: film, theatre, literature, and especially music, as well as through lectures, workshops and meetings. Thanks to the Festival, Jewish culture has returned to Kazimierz and interest in the Kraków Jewish district has been growing steadily.

In 1993 the Judaica Foundation established the Center for Jewish Culture (see Route 1), which through numerous lectures, conferences and seminars, concerts, film showings, and educational programmes aims to disseminate knowledge of the history, culture and religion of the Jews, to preserve the Jewish heritage in the Kazimierz district of Kraków, and to create a platform for Polish-Jewish dialogue. Since 1996 in the first month of the Jewish year – *Tishri* (Sept./Oct.) – *Beit Hadash*, the New Month, has taken place – the Month of Encounters with Jewish Culture, usually devoted to one personage (e.g. Franz Kafka or Mordechai Gebirtig) or a specific topic (Jewish Galicia). Until quite recent-

The idea of the Jewish Culture Festival in Kraków originated from our genuine fascination with the world of Jewish culture. In the course of time it has transformed into a deepened reflection on the history, culture and religion of the Jewish nation. Jews developed their own culture and art here over centuries – for nearly a thousand years. But also in this place, Shoah *[the Holocaust] marked its tragic end. We are painfully aware of this every day. We have inherited remembrance of the history and cultural heritage of the Jewish nation. The Festival is the celebration of Jewish life, art and culture. It is the victory of life over death. And like* Kaddish, *it is a symbol for the remembrance of the death of millions of Jews from all over the world. ... Once a year we experience the gift of being in the united world of* Shalom. *The centre of that world is Kazimierz – the Jewish quarter of Kraków.*

Janusz Makuch and Krzysztof Gierat,
the originators of the Jewish Culture Festival

ly, the late Rafael Scharf came back here, after "years stormy and turbulent, to cast an eye over the landscape of my youth and my childhood, where every stone is laden with sweet memories, to walk through the streets where our fates intermingled, where the Street of Corpus Christi crossed with the Street of Rabbi Meisels, and the Street of Saint Sebastian with that of Berek Joselewicz. (*As in a dream*)"

Also in 1993 Steven Spielberg filmed *Schindler's List* in Kazimierz, which was an eye-opener in many parts of the world on the tragedy that happened here. Moreover, more and more people have returned to Kazimierz – some come here to see the places where the movie was made; others come here to seek their roots or absorb the unique atmosphere of those amazing corners connected with the history and culture of the Kraków Jews.

Soon afterwards the first Jewish bookshop, 'Jarden', was established in Kazimierz, boasting many publications on Jewish history, culture, religion and tradition. The bookshop, a tourist agency at the same time, was the first to offer the *Schindler's List* guided tour to tourists arriving in Kazimierz.

Since the early 1990s the Ronald S. Lauder Foundation has been present in Kazimierz. It aims at the preservation and protection of Jewish heritage, charity and cultural work for the Jewish community, supporting initiatives aiming to create new possibilities of Polish-Jewish dialogue and to present its educational programmes to anyone who has a Jewish background.

It was then that the 'Social and Cultural Association of Jews' was reactivated. In 1995 the Jewish congregation numbered about 160. The community retrieved sovereign rights to administer historical sacred buildings, which have been recently renovated. With the financial contribution of the National Fund for Monuments Protection and private sponsors, the Isaac Synagogue and the Kupa Synagogue have been renovated, the Tempel Synagogue has been restored to its former glory, and the Old Synagogue has been maintained in good condition. Since 1997 Kraków has again been hosting a rabbi.

Since the early 1980s the anniversary of the Kraków ghetto liquidation has been celebrated by a March of Remembrance. Although in previous years only a handful of people partook in it, recently it has had a better turnout. In 2003, on the 60th anniversary of the liquidation of the Kraków ghetto, several hundred people followed the route along which the Germans had driven Jews to the Płaszów camp. Each of the participants received a photocopy of the *kenkart* [ID] of a former ghetto inhabitant, with whom they identified during the march. The march ended at the monument commemorating the Jewish victims at the site of the former Płaszów Camp, where *Kaddish*, a Jewish mourner's prayer, and Psalm 130 were recited, and according to the Jewish custom stones were placed there.

In 2002 at Nowy Square the 1st International Soup Festival, following the example of the French Soup Festival in Lille, was organised. This unusual event attracted hundreds of Cracovians eager to taste over 60 kinds of soups prepared both by professional cooks and amateurs. Having tried all soups, the Festival Jury chooses the best three. Most pubs, restaurants and cafés take part in the Festival, and its atmosphere prevails in soup gourmets' memories for a long time. In 2003 the 2nd International Soup Festival was held under the slogan 'Diversity of Nations, Cultures, Traditions and… Tastes'.

In 2003 a debate on the district's reactivation began between its locals, representatives of various Kazimierz institutions and municipal representatives. Municipal officials and 'friends of Kazimierz', that is artists and businesspeople, worked out a first draft of the new concept of the Kazimierz district. This was a top-down approach, but it is thanks to these grass roots activities that Kazimierz has already been brought to life by a free market and by members of an artistic community full of ideas, energy and enthusiasm.

Walking Tours around Kazimierz

45 — 140

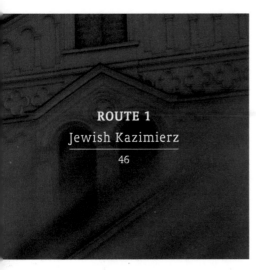

ROUTE 1
Jewish Kazimierz

This route is designed for those who do not have much time but would like to visit the most important historical monuments of Jewish Kazimierz. We shall begin our 3-hour walk through the streets of Kazimierz in ul. Szeroka near the city centre of Kraków (it is a 15-minute walk from the Main Market Square; you can also take trams no. 3, 13, or 24 running along ul. Starowiślna).

1 Landau Mansion
2 the Great Mikvah
3 the Remuh Synagogue
4 the Remuh Cemetery
5 the Oldest Jewish Cemetery in Kazimierz
6 House at no. 14 (Helena Rubinstein's house)
7 the Popper Synagogue
8 the Rabbinical House
9 the Synagogue On the Hill (Auf'n Bergel)
10 the Old Synagogue
11 the Kowea Itim L'tora Prayer House
12 the High Synagogue
13 Parish School
14 Courtyard at ul. Józefa 12
15 Prayer House of the Psalm Brotherhood (Chewra Thilim)
16 Centre for Jewish Culture
17 Ritual Slaughterhouse
18 the Isaac Synagogue
19 the Mizrachi Prayer House
20 the Kupa Synagogue
21 the Talmud Torah School and Prayer House
22 the Reform Synagogue (Tempel)
23 the Handicraft Boarding Workshops
24 the Craft Secondary School
25 the Chaim Hilfstein Hebrew Lower Secondary School
26 the Hebrew Public School
27 the Salomon Daiches Prayer House
28 the Mordechai Gebirtig Memorial Plaque
29 Heder Ivri and Tachkemoni Schools
30 the New Cemetery

■ ul. Szeroka > ul. Józefa > ul. Bożego Ciała > ul. Meiselsa > plac Nowy > ul. Izaaka > ul. Kupa > ul. Warszauera > ul. Estery > ul. Miodowa > ul. Podbrzezie > ul. Brzozowa > ul. Berka Joselewicza > ul. Brzozowa > ul. Miodowa

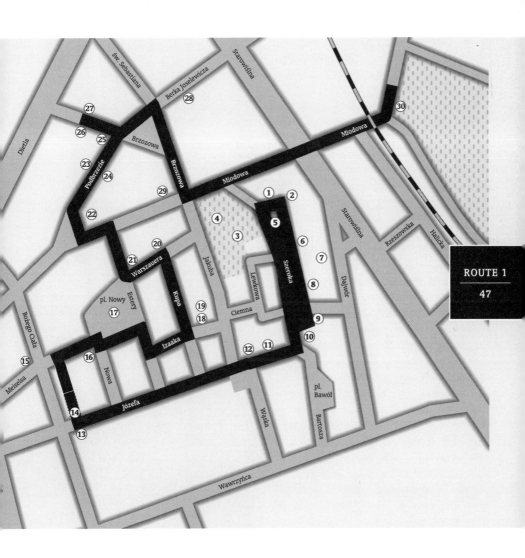

Ul. Szeroka is the very heart of present-day Jewish Kazimierz. It is actually a wide square, which has been the centre of the Jewish town since the 15th century. Its importance is evidenced by the fact that once as many as four synagogues were situated here, which did not occur anywhere else in Europe. Moreover, a few prayer houses, the *kahal* [the Community board] office; the *mikvah*, the ritual bath house, and two cemeteries were located here. Fortunately, Kraków was not bombed during World War II, therefore some parts of Szeroka's urban structure date from the times of the 16th and 17th-century Jewish town, and the street itself is one of the few remaining places in Kraków paved with Austrian cobblestone.

The two-storey Renaissance **LANDAU MANSION**  (ul. Szeroka 2), sometimes erroneously called the Jordans Palace, dates from the 17th century when three magnificent buildings belonging to Doctor Samuel, Moses Yekeles and Wolf Popper were joined into one. Next to the mansion there is the building of the former **GREAT MIKVAH** (ul. Szeroka 6), restored in the 1970s. This ritual bath house must have been established at the turn of the 15th and 16th centuries, although it was first mentioned only in 1567, when the wooden floor collapsed and 10 women drowned. The crowd in the mikvah

Revival of 'Jewish' life in Kazimierz

was likely to be caused by the regulation that when the king was present at Wawel, Jewesses were forbidden to bathe in the Vistula River. The bath house functioned until World War II. Today the building hosts a lovely hotel and restaurant, whereas the only functioning mikvah is located in the cellars of the Eden Hotel.

Walking alongside the wall on our right, we will reach a gate with a Hebrew inscription: "New Synagogue – Blessed Memory of the Remuh". It leads to the courtyard of the **REMUH SYNAGOGUE**. 3 (Attention! Men are obliged to cover their heads while in the synagogue and at the cemetery. Yarmulkes are included in the price of the ticket, available in the synagogue's vestibule). The synagogue was founded in 1553 by Israel (Isserl) ben Joseph, father of Rabbi Moses Isserles (Remuh). It was erected to worship "the Ever-Present, and Isserl's wife, Malke, who died of the plague in 1551-52", as the interior inscription informs. Israel received official royal permission to open the synagogue in 1556. Soon afterwards, in 1557, the Great Fire of Kazimierz consumed the whole of the Jewish town together with the newly opened synagogue. Its present shape is a result of the thorough renovation of 1829. Unfortunately, during the Second World War

Legend of the Remuh Synagogue's Founder

Israel Isserl, founder of the Remuh Synagogue, was a well-known merchant and banker who did a lot of business, especially in Lithuania. A very pious man, he used to close his shop on Friday at noon in order to get ready for the Sabbath, which begins at sunset. As legend has it, one Friday, just before noon, a wealthy merchant came into the shop. Noon arrived and the merchant was still browsing among the numerous goods. Israel approached him and said that he had to close the shop and invited him back after the Sabbath. The merchant replied that there were still a few hours left before the Sabbath was due to start and he was planning to make a huge purchase, since he was about to become a royal supplier and could possibly become Israel's regular customer. "I am sorry, but this is my custom and I shall not change it for all the treasures of this world", explained Israel. The merchant felt insulted, left the shop and never came back. But this deed was noticed in heavenly spheres; and since Israel had such great respect for the Sabbath that he would suffer a loss in profit for it, he was rewarded – soon his son was born, who became the most famous and respected rabbi of Kraków.

H. Halkowski, *Legends of the Jewish Town of Kazimierz near Kraków*, Kraków 1998

The Remuh Cemetery where the great Jewish rabbis rest

it was taken over by the German authorities and turned into military storage rooms, which completely destroyed the synagogue's furnishings. Renovated after World War II at the Jewish Community's expense, it is the only Orthodox synagogue in Kraków offering regular religious services. Its atmosphere cannot be found in any other Kazimierz synagogue. Its size, once a private *shul* for family and friends, gives us an idea of the size of the present Jewish Community in Kraków, which numbers about 100.

The synagogue was not named after the founder, but after his renowned son, Rabbi Moses Isserles (1520-72), usually referred to as 'the Remuh' an acronym of Rabbi Moses Isserles (רמ"ו) 'Remu' (according to Galician pronunciation) or 'Rema'. He studied at the Shalom Shahna Yeshiva of Lublin and was considered a prominent Talmudist while still at school. A boy wonder, he returned from Lublin with a rabbinical certificate and a wife, the young and beautiful Golde, the daughter of his teacher. At the age of 22 the Remuh was appointed chief rabbi of Kraków (in 1542), as well as head of the Yeshiva of Kraków, and held the posts until his death. As a distinguished scholar and one of the greatest authorities, he was also the author of many literary writings on religion, philosophy, mys-

ticism, natural science and Ashkenazic law. What made him renowned all over the Jewish world was a work called *Mappa* [Tablecloth], a codification of the Ashkenazic laws, and a commentary to the Sephardim code of laws called *Shulhan Aruch* [The Laid Table] by Joseph Karo. Both works have been published together as an entity ever since, and have been followed by Orthodox Jews until the present day. Moses Isserles died on *Lag ba-Omer* (see p. 55) – and even now on the anniversary of his death thousands of Jews from all over the world come to pray at his grave. Original elements of the synagogue include the stone money-box (late 16th c.) to the left of the entrance to the main prayer hall with the inscription: "gold, silver, bronze" (Exodus 35: 5), which was meant to encourage donations; and the stone Renaissance *Aron Kodesh*, holy ark, where the Torah, the first five books of the Bible, is stored, placed in the eastern wall (facing Jerusalem) and topped by the Tables of the Decalogue. A *shivviti* tablet with the inscription "I have set the Lord always before me" (Ps.16:8) and "Remember who you face, the King of the kings of kings, the Holy One blessed be He" (Talmud) is customarily placed in front of the cantor's stand. What is astonishing is that the space where the *hazan*, the cantor, stands is lowered in order to fulfil the verse "Out of depths I cry to Thee O Lord"

(Ps.130:1). The plaque on the right of the *Aron Kodesh* commemorates the place where the Remuh used to pray. In the middle of the synagogue we can see the *bimah*, the pulpit from which the Torah is read during the service. The original was destroyed during World War II, and the present one is its exact reconstruction, done in 1958. A pair of wooden doors at the *bimah*, dating from the 17th and 18th centuries, display the furnishings of the Jerusalem Temple. On the southern wall there is a table commemorating the late members of the community, where small lamps are lit during the mourner's prayer. Women are not allowed in the main prayer hall, since their presence would disturb the purity of prayers, and thus a separate gallery for women (with a separate entrance) is located at the back of the synagogue. On the western wall, above the arcade joining the gallery for women with the main prayer hall, we can see 20th-century wall paintings depicting, beginning from the right-hand side: *The Wailing Wall* (The Western Wall of the Temple in Jerusalem – the only remnant of the Temple, destroyed in 70 AD), *Noah's Ark* and *The Tomb of the Matriarch Rachel*.

Having left the synagogue, we pass by the wall on the left with plaques commemorating the Kraków Jews, brought here before 1968 from various buildings in Kazimierz. Through the gate leading to the cemetery, above which there is a Hebrew inscription which reads: "The Old cemetery, a resting place of *Geonim*, established by the kahal in 5311" (i.e. 1552 of the Christian calendar), we enter the **REMUH CEMETERY** 4 . We are immediately overwhelmed by its unique atmosphere: silence and meditation accompanying "the great leaders, legislators and scholars of the Jewish people resting here for centuries", as Rabbi Ber Meisels put it in the 19th century. The cemetery is the oldest preserved Jewish necropolis in Kraków, and one of the oldest in Poland – unique both historically and artistically. The first numerous burials were given in 1552 to the victims of the 1551-1552 plague. The former cemetery gate has also been preserved – it has been walled up but is still visible in the rear brick wall in ul. Jakuba. The cemetery was extended a number of times and finally closed down in 1800 by the Austrian authorities. It was then that the New Cemetery at ul. Miodowa was established (see p. 76). Since then the cemetery has been gradually deteriorating. At the turn of the 19th and 20th centuries the Community took care of the rabbis' graves only. In 1935 Majer Bałaban admitted that the majority of the *matzevas*, tombstones, had vanished, few stones were left and it was almost impossible to read the inscriptions. During the Second

The 'Kraków Wailing Wall'

World War the Nazis turned it into a garbage dump and destroyed the remaining tombstones. In the late 1940s several reconstructed *matzevas* replaced the dilapidated or missing rabbis' tombstones. As an unwritten account has it, just before the outbreak of World War II members of the Jewish Community covered part of the cemetery with a layer of earth. This might be confirmed by the fact that during the cemetery renovation in the late 1950s several hundreds of intact and broken tombstones were unearthed. A number of tombstones considered missing were rediscovered, therefore some rabbis now have two tombstones. The Jewish Community was unable to recreate the original arrangement, therefore over 700 tombstones were placed in rows (which is rather unusual in Eastern European Jewish cemeteries, which are usually characterised by a specific chaos). Thus, in most cases the person described on the tombstone is not the person buried beneath. The broken *matzevas* have been put in the eastern cemetery wall, heading for Jerusalem, which has come to be referred to as the 'Kraków Wailing Wall'.

Two types of tombs are to be admired at the cemetery: sarcophagi and standing tombstones, dating from the second half of the 16th century, among which there are many beautiful Renaissance and Baroque stones. The steel roofs topping the tombstones have nothing

Tombstone symbols – one of the popular motifs are candlesticks present at female tombstones. Women's only religious privilege is to light candles at the beginning of the Sabbath. Scholarly wisdom is often represented by the Torah scrolls or books. Animals are also fairly popular: the deer signifies the name of Hirsch (Yiddish) or Cwi, Naftali (Hebrew), and the impetuous fulfilling of God's will; the bear – the name of Dov (Hebrew) or Ber (Yiddish), the bird – an allegory of soul, the eagle – God's care, the dove – peace, agreement and married love, the stork – wisdom, the pelican – parental love. Apart from these, you can often see a menorah or the Star of David, symbols of Judaism. Mystical or fantastic creatures also appear on the tombstones, such as Leviatans, gryphs, unicorns, and dragons, which are to guard the tomb against evil powers. Floral motifs in form of rosettes, garlands etc. appeared under the influence of Renaissance and Baroque gentile secular arts as purely decorative elements. Death attributes such as a broken tree, torn branch, broken column, snuffed candle or hourglass are also present.

to do with religion; they serve merely as protection against acid rain. The huge grave, piled up with stones opposite the entrance, contains bones that were unearthed during the wall renovation in the 1990s.

From the gate we turn left, follow the pavement and turn left again behind the synagogue. Under a tree, behind a grilled fence, we can see the only tomb that has not been destroyed – **the tomb of Moses Isserles, the Remuh** A . (According to oral tradition, the Germans who tried to destroy the Remuh's tomb were struck by a bolt of lightning from heaven. Religious Jews interpret this legend as a sign of the Remuh's power). The tombstone dates from the second half of the 18th century, whereas the original 16th-century

one is placed at the back. The inscription on the grave contains the famous words: כמשה ממשה ועד משה לא קם [mimoshe ad moshe lo kam kemoshe] "From Moses (the Prophet) to Moses (Isserles) there was no one like Moses", which only reveals the respect he earned among Jews. There are many votive pieces of paper, *kvitleh*, around the tomb, left by pilgrims to the Remuh's tomb, who believe that he will plead with God for them. We can also notice stones placed on top of the tombs as a sign of respect and commemoration by visitors. (According to one interpretation the

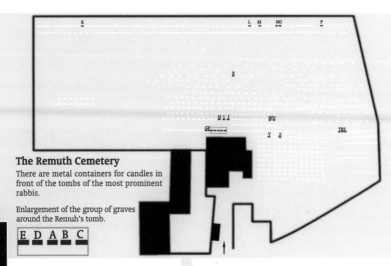

The Remuth Cemetery

There are metal containers for candles in front of the tombs of the most prominent rabbis.

Enlargement of the group of graves around the Remuh's tomb.

E D A B C

tradition of putting stones on tombs originated in Biblical times when Jews wandering through the desert after the Exodus from Egypt put stones over the dead bodies of those who had passed away on the way, in order to mark their graves).

The symbols on the tombstones are worth some attention. On the Remuh's tombstone (and many others) we can see a crown, referring to the verse "there are three crowns: the crown of Torah, the crown of priesthood, and the royal crown, but the crown of a good name excels them all" (Ethics of the Fathers, 4:13). This usually means a profound knowledge of the Torah and piety, but also the de-

ceased's virtues (a good name), who had done much good in their lifetime. On Rabbi Isserles' tombstone we can also see grapes, a symbol of wisdom, knowledge, maturity and spiritual depth, as well as of the people of Israel and nostalgia for the Promised Land. The Remuh is surrounded by members of his family. Next to the Remuh on the right rest: his brother, **Isaac the Rich** B (died 1585), a Community senior of several years standing; and **Joseph Kac** C (died 1591), a prominent Talmudist, head of the Kraków Yeshiva, and brother-in-law of Moses Isserles who, after his first wife's death, married Joseph's sister. Kac's wife, Shprintza, his son, Tanchum, and his

A Tsaddik Miser

One may wonder why the famous 17th century rabbis such as Gershon Saul Yom Tov Lipman Heller, Joel Sirkes, Joshua ben Joseph or Joshua Heshel are buried at the back of the cemetery. Perhaps it is connected with the cemetery entrance gate being replaced twice (in the 16th century the entrance was – as it is today – from ul. Szeroka, but in the 17th century the cemetery was entered from ul. Jakuba) The 17th-century rabbis were buried in the front of it, which today is the very back. Another explanation why Lipman Heller is buried at the back of the cemetery is provided by a legend. In Kazimierz lived a wealthy man who always refused to donate for charity, so that he soon became referred to as 'the Miser of Kraków'. Because he was considered an evil man, when he died he was buried by the wall at the back of the cemetery. On the first Friday after his death all poor citizens of Kazimierz, who had been used to receiving money for the Sabbath from an unknown benefactor, received nothing. It turned out that the 'miser' was the greatest *tsaddik*, or righteous man, since according to Jewish law giving charity anonymously is the greatest virtue. It was for this reason that Rabbi Heller wished to be buried next to him. Thus, the famous rabbi is buried at the back of the cemetery.

H. Halkowski, *Legends of the Jewish Town of Kazimierz near Kraków*, Kraków 1998

grandson, Gershon, are also mentioned on his tombstone. Both tombstones were made after 1945. On Moses Isserles's left lie: his father, the founder of the Remuh Synagogue, **Israel Isserl** D (died 1568), and his sister, **Miriam Bella** E (died 1617). Next to the fence in the same line rest: **Gitel** F (died 1552), Moses Isserles's grandmother, accompanied by his first wife, **Golde** G (died 1552). (Her matzeva is seriously damaged). Behind the fence at the back, on the right, lie: his only daughter, **Drezel** H (died 1622) and his mother, **Malke** I (died 1552). The neighbouring tomb attracts attention due to the shape of its sarcophagus. It is the tomb of **Mordechai Saba**, known as Singer J (died 1576), the Remuh's successor at the Kraków Yeshiva from 1572 to 1576. He was also a renowned expert on Hebrew grammar and Kabala. From the Remuh's tomb we follow the path along Gitel and Golde's tombstones up the hill; we turn right, heading for the rear cemetery wall. Having reached the wall, we turn left, and after several dozen steps we encounter the tomb of **Gershon Saul Yom Tov Lipman Heller** K (1579-1654, see p. 16), prominent Talmudist, rabbi of Vienna, Prague and Kraków from 1643, head of the Yeshiva of Kraków (from 1648). His matzeva has another symbol on it: an ewer and a *laver*, basin, which indicate that it is the tomb of a Levite, one of the descendants of Levi, who were in attendance upon the priests in the Temple, assisting them to wash their hands before the service, among other things (hence the ewer and the basin).

Let us follow the path back along the wall, pass the former cemetery gate on the left and after several metres stop in front of the black marble tombstone, bearing a faintly visible ewer and basin. Here lies **Isaac ben Mordechai Ha-Levi** L (Levite), rabbi, head of the rabbinical court and the Yeshiva of Kraków from 1776 to 1799, and fanatic opponent of the Hasidic Jews, whom he excommunicated twice in 1785 and 1797 in the Old Synagogue (10 tombstones further on there is his second tombstone, made after 1945). Three tombs away from Isaac Ha-Levi's original tombstone rests **Samuel bar Meshulam** M (died 1552) – royal physician of King Sigismund the Old, who arrived in Kraków with the king's wife, the Italian Queen, Bona Sforza, and their son, Sigismund Augustus. The original massive matzeva is rectangular and bears no ornamentation. Four tombstones away lies **Joshua Heshel** N (died 1653), Kraków rabbi and head of the Yeshiva of Kraków from 1654 to 1663. Next to him rests **Joshua ben Joseph** O (1590-1648),

head of the Yeshiva of Kraków and author of *Meggine Shlomo* [Salomon's Shields], the title of which can be seen on the matzeva. (It is next to this tombstone that the second tombstone of Isaac Ha-Levi stands). We continue towards the northern cemetery wall heading for the tombstone of the renowned Kraków rabbi **Joel Sirkes** P (1561-1640), known as BaH after the title of his work (see p. 15), which is located ten tombstones further on (the eighth stone from the wall). We follow the path, turn right and head for the 'Wailing Wall'. On the way we stop at the tombstone of the most famous Kabbalist, **Nathan Nata Spira** R (1583-1633), referred to as *Megalleh Amukkot* [Revealing Depths] after the title of his work (see p. 15), and known as a miracle-maker. The inscription on his grave reads: "here lies a holy man, the most holy of the ancestors, revealing depths [megalleh amukkot], secrets and treasures, he who is said to have spoken to Elijah face to face". We can linger at his tomb, place a stone upon it, and ask for something we truly desire, bearing in mind that those who ask for little, do receive. His wife, **Rose** S (died 1642) rests to his left, and his daughter, **Debora** T (died 1642) to his right. His son is buried two rows away.

Continuing straight on along the path towards the Remuh's tomb, on our right we pass a tombstone with black letters which belongs to **Eliezer Ashkenazi** Ⓤ (1512-85), rabbi of Cairo, Cyprus, a physician and scholar. Customarily, the symbols on the tombstones refer to religious or spiritual aspects of life; however, the snake visible on his *matzeva* is one of two symbols at this cemetery referring to profession. (For an explanation of other tombstone symbols – see box p. 55). The other symbol depicts a pair of scissors and indicates the profession of tailor on the tombstone of Isaac, son of Cwi, known as **Karif Shnaider** Ⓧ (died 1613) – his tomb is located in a straight line from that of Joseph Kac (near the Remuh), in the middle of the path leading to the rear wall of the cemetery. Next to Askhenazy's tomb is the second tombstone of **Isaac Jakubowicz (Reb Isaac reb Yekeles)** Ⓦ, called 'the Rich' (died 1653), merchant, banker, a community senior of several years' standing and the founder of the Isaac Synagogue (see p. 70). The remnant of the original tombstone lies two rows away in the direction of the 'Wailing Wall'. One row in front (the 10th from the 'Wailing Wall') on the 3rd and 5th Ⓨ Ⓩ tombstones from the pavement next to the synagogue, we can see hands raised in a gesture of blessing, indicating the tomb of a priest (*Cohen*). Priests were supposed to have descended from Aaron and used to be God's servants in the Temple in Jerusalem. The symbol is placed only on

Nathan Spira and the Prophet

Nathan Spira's father-in-law was the very influential Moses Jakubowicz (Jekeles), brother of the Isaac Synagogue's founder; who erected a separate synagogue called 'On the Hill' for his son-in-law. Nathan Spira, known as Megalleh Amukkot, worked day and night, but it was not immediately that everyone recognised a great man in him. Moses thought that Nathan was neglecting his wife, became more and more upset with him and told his daughter to divorce him, but Rose refused. One day Nathan told his wife: "I am going to work now, so, please, allow no one to disturb me". At the same time Moses ran out of patience, rushed into his daughter's house and demanded to see his son-in-law at once. Rose begged him not to, because her husband had asked not to be disturbed. It only enraged Moses Jekeles, who dashed into Nathan's study, and... fell dead. There was Nathan Spira talking face-to-face with the Prophet Elijah, who visits only the most distinguished scholars and the sight of whom makes ordinary people fall dead on the spot.

(This legend was told to the author by Reb B. Lappe of London, who is closely tied to Kazimierz and Rabbi Megalleh Amukkot)

The fence of the oldest Jewish Cemetery in Kazimierz in ul. Szeroka

male tombstones and the title of *Cohen* is hereditary. On the 5th tomb from the pavement, apart from the hands we can also see lions standing up on their hind legs, supporting a crown, already familiar to us. Their symbolic meaning has a number of interpretations: a lion was often used as an illustration of the deceased's name – equivalent of 'lion' Judah, *Leib* (in Yiddish), or *Aryel* (in Hebrew); or as a symbol of strength and power. It also referred to the passage "Be as strong as a leopard, light as an eagle, fleet as a hart and brave as a lion to perform the will of thy Father who is in heaven" (Ethics of the Fathers, 5:20). This is the tomb of Isaac Spira (died 1652), son of David, head of the Yeshiva of Kraków. Nevertheless, bearing in mind the meaning of the aforementioned symbols, and not knowing a single word in Hebrew, we could presume that the person buried here was a man (the blessing hands), a scholar with profound religious knowledge (the crown), that he was mighty and powerful, and did his best to fulfil God's will (the lion), that he belonged to a Cohen tribe, (the blessing hands) and must have been a good-hearted man (the crown of a good name).

We leave the cemetery, passing on the right, the 19th-century house of *Shammash*, the synagogue caretaker. Back in ul. Szeroka we head for a little square enclosed with an ornamented fenced.

It was here that the **OLDEST JEWISH CEMETERY IN KAZIMIERZ** 5 , was situated. It was closed down in 1552, when the Remuh Cemetery was opened. The cemetery was adjoined from the north by a shelter house for the poor, demolished in the early 19th century. A monument commemorating the victims of the Holocaust – 65,000 Kraków Jews who died during World War II – is located on the southern end of the square. The legend of an unfortunate wedding is associated with the cemetery, which was held on the Sabbath in a wedding house located here. They say it was in the times of the Remuh (although present-day Remuh cemetery had already existed then), who came out of the synagogue and admonished the wedding guests for breaking the rules of the Sabbath. However, they ignored him, so he excommunicated them and soon the earth opened up and swallowed the newlyweds together with the guests, and the cemetery was established. According to other sources, it was only the newlyweds who died. The legend explains the local prohibition on holding weddings on the Sabbath in Kraków, though such legends occur in many Jewish towns of southeastern Poland.

We head for the Old Synagogue. On our left we pass the **HOUSE AT NO 14** 6 , where Helena (Chaye) Rubinstein (1870-1965), the "queen of cosmetics", was born. Pablo Picasso described her as: "As ingenious as me (...because she has

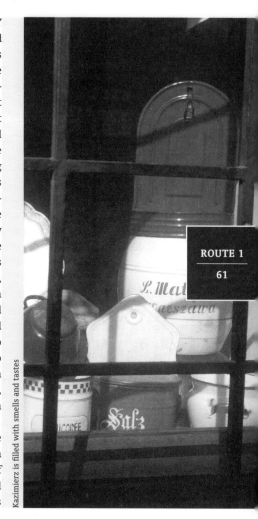

Kazimierz is filled with smells and tastes

the same huge ears)". Aged 20, she emigrated to Australia, where she began selling a cream made according to a formula of her mother's meant to improve the dry skin of Australian women. In 1900 she moved to London, where she opened a fashionable salon in Mayfair, which, like the Melbourne salon, became extremely popular. In 1912 she opened a salon in Paris and in 1915 she set out to conquer America. After World War I she was considered Europe's leading cosmetician, and her products, despite the competition of Canadian Elizabeth Arden and Austrian Ester Lauder, sold extremely well. Shortly before the Stock Market Crash of 1929 she sold her empire to the Lehman Brothers Company for 8 mln dollars, only to buy it back in 1930 for... 2 mln dollars. When asked how she had managed to earn 6 mln dollars so easily, she answered, "It only involved slight impudence". Charming and energetic, she was part of the international social elite. As an art collector and patron of the arts she established the Helena Rubinstein Foundation, which supports museums, schools and young artists.

At no. 16 the **POPPER SYNAGOGUE** 7 (also known as the Stork's Synagogue) is located. It was erected in 1620 by Wolf Popper, an eminent merchant and banker, whose name was known to wide circles of the trading world in Europe. He was believed to stand on one leg while meditating, hence his nickname 'Stork'. According to Bałaban: "Wolf Stork was one of the wealthiest, or perhaps the wealthiest, Jew in Kraków". The synagogue was situated at the back of a courtyard, and adjoined the Kazimierz city wall from the east. The small, rectangular synagogue, with a gallery for women in the annex on the northwestern side, was one of the richest synagogues. It has been taken over by the Community over the course of time. During the Second World War the whole of its furnishings was destroyed, except for the holy ark door, at present exhibited at the Sir Isaac and Lady Edith Wolfson Museum in Jerusalem. After the war it no longer functioned as a synagogue. After the renovation of 1965 it was taken over by the Old Town Youth Cultural Centre, and now it hosts the Atelier Gallery, the Children and Youth Art Workshops Studio, and European Education Centre.

At no. 18 a non-existing building (the present one is much younger) used to host the **RABBINICAL HOUSE** 8, where a Kraków rabbi, Isaac Ha-Levi, lived between 1776 and 1799, who could not bear the Hasidic Jews and excommunicated them twice. The plot between the Old Synagogue and the building at no. 22 once belonged to Isaac Yekeles the Rich, who founded the Isaac Synagogue (see p. 70). His brother, Moses Yekeles, erected here the **SYNAGOGUE 'ON THE HILL'** 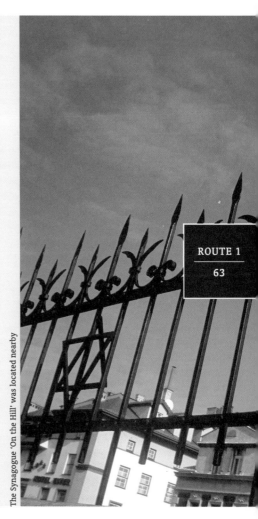 (*Auf'n Bergel*) for his son-in-law, the eminent Kabalist Nathan Nata Spira (Megalleh Amukkot). Actually, it was a *beit ha-midrash* adjacent to a yeshiva, which was situated on the top floor (hence the name), with a small *mikvah* in the cellars. The synagogue was demolished during World War II. "A tradition has it" – according to Bałaban – "that Nathan Spira spent every night in his study, carefully studying Kabalist writings, and the candle in his attic window was like a lighthouse over the dark sea of the Jewish town. Once the candle went out and that night the holy man passed away, on 13th of *Av*, 1633". However, until this very day, when you look up at the attic of the building here you shall see a candle burning in the window, for Kabbalist rabbis do not 'die' in Kraków's Kazimierz.

We face the oldest preserved synagogue in Poland – the **OLD SYNAGOGUE** 10. It was erected in the early 15th century (which is indicated by an original money-box with the year 1407 on it) and was the first synagogue in Kazimierz. Its shape resembles (two-aisled prayer hall with Gothic ribbed vaults) synagogues in Regensburg and Prague. The synagogue is adjacent to the city wall, the reconstructed remnant of which can be seen to the left. Initially, women were not admitted

The Synagogue 'On the Hill' was located nearby

ROUTE 1

63

to the synagogue – the gallery for women on the western side and the vestibule with a well for washing hands on the northern side were added in the early 16ᵗʰ century. The synagogue burnt down during the Great Fire of Kazimierz in 1557, and by 1570 it had been rebuilt by the Italian architect Mateo Gucci, who added a Renaissance touch to it (the walls were topped by an arcade attic, and in the interior he kept Gothic vaults supported by two Tuscan columns). At the turn of the 16ᵗʰ and the 17ᵗʰ centuries – a prayer hall for women, topped by triangle roofs on the northern side, and the 'cantors' hall' on the southern side, which also served as a gallery for women, were added. The synagogue burnt down a few more times: in 1623, 1643, 1693 and 1773. It was restored (1904-13) by Zygmunt Hendel, who gave it a neo-Renaissance look and added a beautiful loggia on the western side. The annex on the northwestern side hosted – according to Bałaban's description of 1935 – the *kahal* office, the Community archives, and a Jewish museum. During the Second World War it shared the fate of other Kazimierz synagogues: its furnishings were destroyed and it was turned into a storage room (the vaults collapsed). In the years 1956-59 it was renovated and adapted for museum purposes and leased to the Historical Museum

The Old Synagogue – the first synagogue in Kazimierz

of Kraków, which established the Museum of Judaism, which hosts a permanent exhibition on the traditions and history of the Kraków Jews, in addition to many temporary exhibitions that are held here. In front of the synagogue there is a monument commemorating 30 Poles murdered here by the Germans in 1943. We enter through the former vestibule; in the left corner we can still see the former well of 'clean water'. We descend the steps to the main prayer hall (the reason why the level of the floor was lowered was a regulation that synagogues should not exceed churches in altitude), we can see a reconstructed 12-angled *bimah*, and a late Renaissance *Aron Kodesh* with a beautifully carved crown above an ornamented door of forged iron. In the former 'cantor's hall' fragments of floral polichromy are still visible. One can admire outstanding Hanukkah lamps, a Torah mantle, pointers in the shape of a hand (*yad*), fine spice-boxes, and paintings on Jewish subjects by Maurycy Gottlieb, Artur Markowicz, Józef Mehoffer, Jacek Malczewski and others. This was the community synagogue, and together with the adjacent *kahal* office it played the role of religious-administrative centre. "It was ... a centre of Jewish life" – declares Bałaban – "since it was here that the most respected members of the community, and

above all rabbis and heads of the Yeshiva of Kraków prayed. Weddings were held in its courtyard, royal, voivodship and senioral regulations were announced from the *bimah*, and rabbinical excommunications were cast at the disobedient citizens. Here gathered the Community in times of prosperity and adversity, and here they pleaded to God when a plague was approaching or a drought threatened with crop failure and famine". It was here that the zealous rabbi Isaac Ha-Levi excommunicated the Hasidic Jews in 1786 and 1797. It was here that in 1794 Tadeusz Kościuszko gave a speech inviting Jews to partake in the Insurrection against the Russian rule. It was here that Rabbi Dov Ber Meisels appealed for participation in the Uprisings and solidarity with the fighters. It was here that in 1927 the president of Poland, Ignacy Mościcki, paid a visit. Thus, the synagogue also had its political significance, inseparably connected with common Christian-Jewish history and culture.

We leave the Old Synagogue, turn left and walk along the fence. On the left-hand side an amazing loggia with tiny pitchers topping the columns attracts our attention. We turn right into ul. Józefa. The present name of the street does not come from the biblical Joseph, but from Austrian emperor Joseph II, who visited "the province freshly seized from Poland"

and stayed in the mansion on the corner of Józefa and Krakowska streets, known as the Voivode's; and in order to commemorate this event the street obtained its present name. On the right we pass by the **KOWEA ITIM L'TORA PRAYER HOUSE** , at no. 42, that belonged to the Torah Studying Society. On the face of the building we see two Stars of David with the dates of foundation (1810) and restoration (1912), as well as the Hebrew name of the Prayer House. In the adjacent building at no. 40 a *kahal* scribe, Pinkhas Horowitz, lived between 1770 and 1790. There was a *kahal* archive in his house, which almost entirely burnt down in the fire of 1773.

We reach the **HIGH SYNAGOGUE** . The third synagogue to be erected in Kazimierz, between 1556 and 1563, its name is due to the fact that the prayer hall was situated on the first floor for safety reasons, since the main gate to the Jewish town was located at the crossroads of Józefa and Jakuba Streets, next to the house at no. 36.

The synagogue was richly furnished; however, it was completely destroyed during World War II. In 1969-1971 the synagogue was connected with the building at no. 40 and adapted for the Maintenance of Kraków Monuments Committee Studio, which was located here until the late 1990s. Across the street, at no. 33, a building once stood that hosted the very first

The High Synagogue

The loveliest courtyard in Kazimierz where the time has stopped

Hasidic prayer house in Kazimierz, established in 1815 by Kalman Epstein, who is buried at the New Cemetery (ul. Miodowa) and referred to as 'Reb Aron Klojz' after Kalman's son, Aron Epstein, who was in charge of the house until his death in 1882.

We walk along ul. Józefa, which has preserved its unique atmosphere of a small town. Instead of the former shops and workshops, we have the galleries, antique shops, as well as lovely cafés and restaurants. The buildings on the left side of the street belonged to the Augustinian Canons. The house at no. 11 hosted the **PARISH SCHOOL** 13 of the Corpus Christi Church. Its students often pestered the Jews walking by, which often ended in brawls and trials.

Having entered the gate at **UL. JÓZEFA 12** 14, we immediately find ourselves in a completely different world. This picturesque courtyard, one of the most stunning in Kazimierz, was first photographed by Ignacy Krieger in the 1880s, and what is astonishing is that not much has changed since then (apart from its commercialisation, unfortunately). From 1802 W. Luxemburg and M. Wohl had an inn here. We cross the courtyard and stop at a very unusual street corner: the crossroads of Meiselsa and Corpus Christi Streets, which has great symbolic significance. Just as a Jewish street crosses here with a Christian street, so the lives of two na-

Dow Ber Meisels (1798-1870)

An Orthodox Kraków rabbi, a descendant of the Remuh, advocate of Jewish cooperation with the Polish independence movement. He established a bank and a trading partnership, thanks to which he was able to arrange weapon supply for the Polish Uprising of November (1830-31) against the Russian rule. In 1848 he became a delegate for the Vienna parliament. His sharp reply of *"Juden haben keine Recht(s)"* [Jews have no rights] to the speaker of the Austrian parliament, who had asked him why he sat with the Leftists, had become renowned. He supported plenty of charity initiatives and organisations; he was extremely wealthy and distributed the whole of his rabbinical salary to charitable institutions, thus gaining the esteem of the masses. However, the wealthier parts of the society – both the Hasidic and Orthodox – loathed him. In 1856 he was appointed a Warsaw rabbi and always referred to himself as "a Kraków rabbi residing in Warsaw".

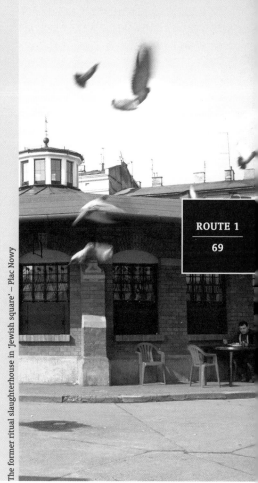

The former ritual slaughterhouse in 'Jewish square' – Plac Nowy

tions crossed in Kazimierz. The corner building (Meiselsa 18 and Bożego Ciała 13), erected in 1896, housed the **PRAYER HOUSE OF THE PSALM BROTHERHOOD** 15 (*Chevra Thilim*). We turn right into ul. Meiselsa, and stop in front of the **CENTER FOR JEWISH CULTURE** 16, which was ceremoniously opened in 1993 (see p. 42). Previously, the 1886 building hosted the *B'nei Emuna* (Sons of Faith) *Beit ha-Midrash*; between 1990-1993 it was thoroughly renovated.

We head for Nowy Square, colloquially known as 'Jewish Square', with a round building in the middle, erected in 1900 as a trade hall, which hosted the **RITUAL SLAUGHTERHOUSE FOR FOWL** 17 between 1927 and 1939. We go along the right side of the square towards ul. Izaaka. Ul. Izaaka ends with the huge **ISAAC SYNAGOGUE** 18 founded by the aforementioned Isaac Jakubowicz (Reb Isaac reb Yekeles) following his wife, Brayndla's, suggestion, according to the inscriptions inside. One of the most famous Hasidic legends that has become a philosophical tale is associated with Isaac. It was often told by Martin Buber and Mircea Eliade. It tells the story of a pious Jew, named Isaac reb Jekeles, who once lived in the Jewish town of Kazimierz. Although he was very poor and had a large family to provide for, he worked hard and never stopped praising God. One day he had a dream that there was a huge treasure buried near a bridge in Prague. Without thinking twice, he went to Prague, which after all is not so far away. When he finally arrived there, he found the bridge he saw in his dream, but it was surrounded by soldiers (some local fights?), so Isaac, son of Jacob, was pondering what to do, when one of the soldiers came over and asked him what he was doing there. Isaac thought that if the worst came to the worst he would split the treasure between them, so he told the soldier about his dream and that the reason he had come there was to check whether the treasure was there. The soldier laughed and replied: "Only such a silly person as you would have done this! Guess what – I've been having a dream for a long time now that in the house of a Kraków Jew named Isaac, son of Jacob, under a stove, a treasure is hidden, but I'm not so stupid as to go there and check. Especially since every second Jew is called Isaac, and every third one – Jacob!" Isaac thanked him, returned home, pulled down the stove and found a great treasure! He then became the richest Jew in Kazimierz, and when asked about the source of his wealth, he answered: "There are things you look for all over the world, and eventually find in your own house. However, to find that out, you need to travel a long way and search far away from home", (According to: H. Halkowski, *Legends of the Jewish Town of Kazimierz near Kraków*, Kraków 1998). Thus is the legend con-

ROUTE 1

70

cerning Isaac, and as far as the synagogue's history is concerned, Isaac received permission from the king to erect a synagogue in 1638; however, due to strong protests from the Corpus Christi parish priest, Rev. Marcin Kłoczyński "There are Catholics living in the neighbourhood and it might happen that a priest may pass by with the Holy Communion", and Bishop Jakub Zadzik, the synagogue was opened only in 1644. A massive early Baroque building, very likely to have been erected by Giovanni Battisto Trevano, with a stunning stucco ceiling that was probably made by Giovanni Battisto Falconi, has continued to make a great impression up until the present day. Initially, the entrance to the synagogue led from ul. Izaaka, where we can still admire a fine 17th-century portal. A gallery for women is situated on the western side, adjoined with the main prayer hall by arcades with Tuscan columns. The loggia is considered one of the most magnificent in Kraków. In 1656, during the Swedish invasion, the synagogue was raided and plundered. In 1924 the outside symmetrical stairs were added, and until 1939 a fish market was located in front of the synagogue. In 1939 Maximilian Redlich, a member of the Community, was shot here because he had refused to set fire to the synagogue. During World War II the interior was devastated and all its furnishings lost. From the mid-1950s until 1969 it was used as a sculpting studio

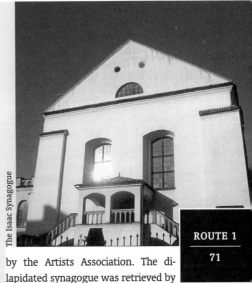

The Isaac Synagogue

by the Artists Association. The dilapidated synagogue was retrieved by the Jewish Community of Kraków in 1989 and renovated in 1994/1995, when marvellous wall paintings were uncovered. At present we can visit the exhibition entitled *In Memory of Polish Jews*, and see two documentaries on the wartime period: *The Removal to the Cracow Ghetto*, 1941, and *The Jewish District of Cracow*, 1936, the latter taking us into the world that has ceased to exist.

From the north, the Isaac Synagogue is adjoined by the **MIZRACHI PRAYER HOUSE** 19, erected in 1924, recently renovated, associated with Orthodox Zionists, which has been hosting the

Ronald R. Lauder Foundation Centre since the early 1990s (see p. 43). At the end of the street we can see the **KUPA SYNAGOGUE** 20, which was established with the *kahal* funds (*mi-kupat-ha-kahal*), hence its name, although it used to be called the Hospital Synagogue – after the hospital situated at the corner of Plac Nowy and ul. Warszauera until the beginning of the 19th century, – or the Poor People's Synagogue. The erection of the building was begun in the 16th century, but it was finished only in 1647. The northern wall of the synagogue was adjacent to the city wall, and from the east the synagogue neighboured on a ritual slaughter house, located on the corner of ul. Jakuba opposite the Remuh Cemetery wall. In the 1830s it was thoroughly renovated. In the interwar period the main prayer hall was covered with stunning polichromy depicting the Wailing Wall, a bird's-eye view of Jerusalem, etc. During the Second World War the synagogue was devastated, but it was reopened just after the war and it was this synagogue that witnessed a pogrom on 11th August, 1945 (see p. 38). Soon afterwards the synagogue was closed down, and one of the halls was turned into a ritual fowl slaughter-house, open till the *shohet*, Abraham Lesman's, death (1985). In 2000-01 a thorough restoration was conducted, funded by the National Fund for Restoration of Kraków Monuments.

How the 'Dead' Saved the Synagogue

When, after a huge effort and many difficulties, Reb Isaac opened the Isaac Synagogue, many people gathered to admire the beauty of the building and the expensive silverware and curtains with which the founder had endowed it. The wealth had not escaped the attention of the town mob, who decided to raid the synagogue and plunder it. A boy warned Reb Isaac and he immediately called on Rabbi Heller after the prayer and asked his advice. The wise rabbi ordered people to close the gates to the Jewish Town and double guard them. Since it was very likely that the raiders would enter the town through the cemetery, he sent for 26 brave Jews, instructed them to dress in white death shirts and to arm themselves with clubs. That night the raiders tried to invade the town, but finding the gate closed, clambered over the cemetery wall to enter the town through the cemetery. To their terror, they saw the 'dead' in white shirts forming a line in front of the rabbis' graves. Petrified by this sight, they took to their heels, and the 'dead' ones chased them with their clubs and seriously battered them. From then on Reb Isaac was left alone and could pray to the Lord in his own synagogue for the remaining nine years of his life.

M. Bałaban, History...

Jonathan Warschauer (1820-88), a doctor, philanthropist and publicist; took part in the Revolution of 1848 that spread across Europe, one of the originators of the Kraków Doctors' Society, from 1866 town councillor. Advocate of assimilation, he helped found the Progressive Israeli Society and erect the Tempel Synagogue. He was deeply involved in charity activity in Kazimierz; buried at the New Cemetery in ul. Miodowa (see p. 78).

Next to the synagogue we can notice another remnant of the city wall that once surrounded Kazimierz – we saw the first one next to the Old Synagogue, and now we may get an idea of how 'big' Kazimierz once was.

We continue along ul. Warszauera, once called Poor Street (after its inhabitants), heading for Plac Nowy. The building on the corner of Estery and Warszauera Streets hosted, from 1813, an Orthodox school, the **TALMUD TORA** 21, financed by a Brotherhood of the same name that also had its prayer house here. In front of us there is a remarkable view of the former ritual slaughterhouse with the tower of Corpus Christi Church in the background – another, as it were, symbol of Jewish-Christian co-existence in Kazimierz. The borders of the Jewish town (by 1822) are clearly visible from here: looking clockwise we start from the east – ul. Warszauera: the city walls spread behind ul. Szeroka situated behind the Remuh Cemetery (we are looking at the cemetery wall); from the south: ahead of us we can see ul. Józefa, which together with ul. św. Wawrzyńca, constituted another border; from the west: behind the building of the Center for Jewish Culture (with a green glass roof), along ul. Bożego Ciała, lay another border; from the north: ul. Miodowa, towards which we shall go now. We turn right into ul. Estery, named not after the biblical Ester but after the aforementioned Jewish Esterka, whose incredible beauty and intelligence captured the heart of King Casimir (see p. 93).

Then we turn left, heading for the youngest and the most magnificent Kazimierz synagogue – the **REFORM SYNAGOGUE** 22, known as the Tempel. It was raised between 1860 and 1862 through the efforts of the Religious-Civilisation Society; in the 1890s it was rebuilt, when a pentagonal apse, and neo-Renaissance ark, resembling the altar in a Christian church, were added. The wooden gallery for women, supported by cast iron pillars, circles the main

The youngest and most beautiful synagogue – the Reform 'Temple'

prayer hall from three sides (north, west and south) and has a U-shape. The beautiful wall paintings, mainly Moorish in style, as well as the stained glass windows, contribute to the synagogue's outstanding charm. During World War II it was destroyed and turned into a storage room, and the northern part into horse stables. Soon after the war, services were held in the Tempel, attended also by traditionalists (hence the *bimah* in the synagogue), in the northern annex a small *mikvah* was established, as well as a prayer hall for the Orthodox in one of the buildings in the garden. After 1968 services were held here sporadically, only to nearly cease in the mid-1980s. The services conducted in the Reform Synagogue had a rather revolutionary character: every week sermons were given, not only in Hebrew (the holy language of services in Orthodox synagogues), but in Polish and German, by distinguished, highly educated preachers. Among them was the aforementioned Osias Thon, who preached here for nearly 30 years. Furthermore, the services here were accompanied by organ music and choir singing (unthinkable in an Orthodox synagogue!), and women were allowed in the choirs. In the late 1990s the building's renovation was sponsored by the World Monuments Fund and the National Fund for Renovation of Kraków Monuments, as well as individual sponsors. It is in this synagogue that the opening concert of the Jewish Culture Festival takes place annually.

Having left the synagogue, we turn right and walk along ul. Podbrzezie. On the way we pass the house at no. 6, where the **HANDICRAFT BOARDING WORKSHOPS** 23 for Jewish orphans were located. The plaque visible on the façade commemorates Sinai (Zygmunt) Aleksandrowicz (1877-1946), a Kraków city councillor, renowned Kraków philanthropist and head of the Boarding Workshops. Opposite this, there used to be the **CRAFT SECONDARY SCHOOL** 24 for boys. The corner building at Podbrzezie and Brzozowa Streets housed **THE CHAIM HILFSTEIN LOWER SECONDARY SCHOOL** 25 (ul. Podbrzezie 8-10); and the **HEBREW PUBLIC SCHOOL** 26 (elementary school, Brzozowa 5). The plaques placed at the corner building with inscriptions in Polish and Hebrew commemorate the schools' existence and their tragic ending in 1939. General subjects were taught in Polish, whereas Jewish subjects were taught in Hebrew. The schools boasted an excellent staff, including Samuel Stendig, philologist, buried at the New Cemetery; Benzion Rappaport, mentioned by Raphael Scharf in his memoirs; Benzion Katz, Hebrew lecturer at the Jagiellonian University; and Hirsh Sherer, mathematician. Several metres away, at ul. Brzozowa 6, there is the eclectic building of the former **SALOMON DAICHES PRAYER HOUSE** `27`, erected in 1910. In nearby ul. Berka Joselewicza (which, mind you, crosses with ul. Św. Sebastiana), at no. 5, the most distinguished Yiddish bard, Mordechai Gebirtig, lived, which is commemorated by a **PLAQUE** `28`.

From ul. Berka Joselewicza we return to ul. Brzozowa and turn into ul. Miodowa. We can pop to the right for a moment to have a glance at the former building of the **HEDER IVRI AND TAKHEMONI SCHOOLS** `29` at no. 26. Erected in 1929 at the Orthodox Zionists' initiative, it was turned into a shelter house for the Jews returning here after 1945.

We turn back and walk along ul. Miodowa, cross ul. Starowiślna, and go under a rail viaduct at the end of ul. Miodowa until we reach the gate of the **NEW CEMETERY** `30`, on the right. Next to the entrance we can see a 19th-century funeral house. This is the largest and the only currently functioning Jewish cemetery in Kraków. It was established in 1800 and covers an area of 19 hectares. Despite its being expanded a number of times, it was filled up during the interwar period. During World War II the cemetery was devastated, the tombstones used as building material, and the more precious tombstones were sold, while the remainder were razed to the ground. According to Bieberstein, in 1944 tomb-

Mordechai Gebirtig (Mordechai Markus Bertig; 1877-1942), Yiddish poet born in Kraków to a poor family; abandoned his education at a religious *heder* and worked as a carpenter and furniture restorer at his brother's workshop in ul. Starowiślna. In 1920 his first collection of poems, *Folkstimlech*, was published. He attained worldwide fame as a Yiddish bard, composing both words and melodies for his songs, e.g. *Hulyet Hulyet Kinderlech* (*Rejoice Children*) and *Kinderyorn* (*Childhood Years*), *Gebirtiga's Mayne lider* (*My Songs*) – 54 songs with notes, including the renowned *Reyzele*, *Undser Shtetl Brent* (*Our Town is Burning* – see box p. 37), which is said to have been written shortly after the pogrom in the town of Przytyk, and became the hymn of the Jewish resistance movement, and *Farewell, my Kraków* (see p. 4). He was shot by the Nazis on 4th June, 1942 in the Kraków ghetto on the way to the railway station. Extremely sensitive, he composed songs that were sung throughout the Jewish world, although they were not associated with his authorship. This may be illustrated by the following anecdote: a street singer was singing Gebirtig's own song *Kinderyorn* (some say it was *Reysele*) beneath his window. When Gebirtig could no longer put up with all the alterations and wanted to correct the singer, the latter bridled at him: "Well, well, I have been singing this song since the Temple was destroyed and he wants to teach me!"

stones were destroyed, the graves opened, and bones and sacred items scattered all over the ground. In 1957 the New Cemetery was renovated with funding from the Joint Distribution Committee. Near the gate on the right, where the members of the Cohen tribe were once buried, there is a **monument commemorating the Jews murdered between 1939 and 1945 by the Hitlerites** A. It is made of broken tombstones and plaques mentioning individual people and whole families (e.g. there is a plaque commemorating the last president of the Jewish Community prior to the war, Dr **Rafał Landau**, and his wife **Rachel**, who died in 1941). The monument is topped by a menorah, symbol of Judaism. Many broken *matzevas* have been placed in the wall, as in the Remuh Cemetery. The newest tombs are located to the right of the monument, on elevated ground. We turn left, towards the main alley near the funeral house. On the way, we pass the tomb of **Abraham Fogel** B (died 1984), cantor in the Remuh Synagogue, buried next to the last cantor of the Tempel Synagogue and ritual slaughterer, **Abraham Lesman** C (died 1985). The oldest preserved tombstones date from the 1840s. They have traditional semicircular coping and are ornamented with numerous magnificent symbols. However, starting from the early 20th century, the tombstones have gradual-

The New Cemetery

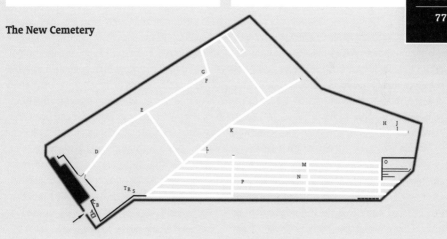

ly lost their Jewish character and have begun to resemble Christian ones, deprived of traditional ornamentation. More and more bilingual Polish-German or Polish-Hebrew tombstones have appeared, as well as stones with German inscriptions only. Walking along the main alley, on the left we shall see the tombs of: **Maciej Jakubowicz** D (died 1979) and his son, **Czesław Jakubowicz** (died 1997), presidents of the Jewish Community in the post-war period. Further to the left, there is the tomb of the aforementioned **Dr Osias Thon** E (1870-1936), a prominent figure of interwar Jewish Kraków – distinguished preacher, rabbi of the 'Tempel' Reform Synagogue, Zionist movement leader, long-term president of the Zionist Organisations of Western Galicia, as well as national parliament deputy, publicist in *Nowy Dziennik* and founder of the 'Ezra' Judaic Library in Kraków (1899) and the Institute of Judaism in ul. Tłomackie in Warsaw (1926) – in other words: the leader of the Kraków Jews in the interwar period. We walk on and several metres ahead, on the right, there is the tomb of **Aron Kirschner** F (1849-1908), head of the Israeli hospital in Kraków. Opposite him is the tomb of **Samuel Stendig** G (died 1942), philologist, political writer propagating Zionist ideas, teacher at the Hebrew Lower Secondary School and head of the Jewish Trade School of Kraków. We continue along the al-

ley, which now makes a large circle. At the first crossroads we turn right, and at the next crossroads left. We walk towards the end of the alley to see the tomb of **Maurycy Gottlieb** H (1856-79), outstanding painter and poet, a student of Jan Matejko. The poem on the obelisk ornamented with a palette reads: "Sublime songs he painted with hues/ For brothers he truly loved/ Death tore him out of this world too early/The world has remembered him". A few steps further on we can see another tombstone in the form of an obelisk, that of **Jonathan Warschauer** I (1820-88), physician and great philanthropist, after whom one of the Kazimierz streets has been named. Behind the obelisk, we can see the bilingual tombstone of **Ignacy Krieger** J (1817-89), photographer, who left magnificent images of 19th-century Kraków (and Kazimierz), its architecture, art, panoramic views and portraits of inhabitants, which enable us to make an unusual 'journey in time'. We return along the same alley, admiring outstanding tombstone symbols on the way. We can see amazing lions, crowns, gryphons, candlesticks and ewers. (For tombstone symbol meanings – see box p. 55). Shortly before the next path crossing, on the left, the Hasidic rabbi, **Shimon Schreiber (Sofer)** K is buried, a Kraków rabbi from 1860 to 1883. We turn left and walk on until the first left turning, at the corner of which the last Kraków rabbi prior to World War II is buried,

Joseph Nechem Kornitzer **L** (rabbi from 1925, died 1933), grandson of the above-mentioned Rabbi Schreiber; and his son, Samuel Shmelkes Kornitzer, murdered in Auschwitz in 1940 (his ashes are buried here). We continue straight on along the path, and on the way we can go astray among the tombs for a while and turn right in order to admire outstanding tombstone symbols: lions, deer, birds and crowns (a row of recently renovated tombstones). We turn left into a path behind the Kornitzers' tomb and after several metres we come across the tomb of **Józef Nüssenfeld** **M** (died 1956), the aforementioned distinguished surgeon, head of the Jewish Hospital in Kraków and the Main Hospital in the Kraków ghetto. We turn right and in the third row from the wall we can see the tomb of **Artur Markowicz** **N** (1872-1934), painter, who preserved the pastel world of Kraków Jews in his works. If we head away from the entrance, we shall reach another **monument commemorating Holocaust victims** **O** – Jews murdered in nearby villages. On the left, along the wall we notice a row of small *matzevas* commemorating those who died in the First World War. We return towards the entrance gate along the second path from the wall. On the way we pass by the tomb of **Józef Sare** **P** (1850-1929), the first Jewish vice-Mayor of Kraków from 1905 to 1929. We reach an alley joining all parallel paths, we continue along the alley until the bend in the wall, where we turn right and find the tombs of Hasidic tsaddiks: **Kalonimus Kalman Epstein** **R** (died 1823) – disciple of Rabbi Elimelech of Leżajsk, author of *Maor Va-Shemesh*, first supporter of Hasidism in Kraków and founder of the first Hasidic prayer house in 1815, excommunicated twice by the aforementioned Rabbi Isaac Ha-Levi who is buried at the Remuh Cemetery; and on the left is his son, **Aron Epstein** **S** (died 1882), who was the Kraków Hasidic leader until his death. On the right of Kalman's tomb, we can see the beautifully ornamented (lions supporting a grapevine) tomb of **Salomon Zalman Joseph of Wielopole** **T** (died 1857), who did not originate from Kraków, but who always believed that it was good to be near Kalman Epstein, and therefore when he died, while travelling, someone recalled his words and he was buried next to Kalman Epstein.

Our visit to Jewish Kazimierz comes to an end here. In order to gain a lasting impression of the place, we recommend visiting one of the nearby restaurants in ul. Szeroka (Klezmer-Hois, Anatewka, Ariel, Alef or Arka Noego) to regain your strength after such a long, exhausting walk with some delicious Jewish cuisine (see Practical Information). And perhaps muse over Jewish Kazimierz buried in the past...

ROUTE 2
Christian Kazimierz

80

This route takes you along the most important Christian monuments of Kazimierz.
The walking tour lasts about 2 hours.

Wolnica Square > ul. Bożego Ciała > ul. Józefa > ul. św. Katarzyny > ul. Skałeczna > ul. Krakowska > the Marshal Józef Piłsudski Bridge

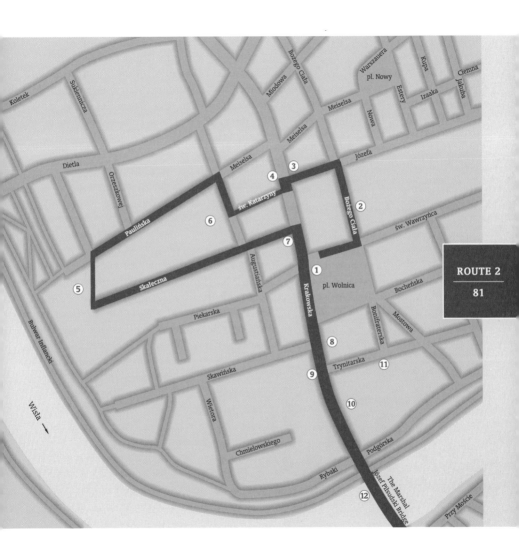

The former town hall of Kazimierz

We begin our walking tour around Christian Kazimierz at the former Kazimierz market square – Wolnica Square. It constitutes merely 1/4 of the previous square, which, laid out in 1335, with dimensions of 195 m x 195 m, was almost as large as the Kraków Main Market Square (see p. 8). Today its initial shape has disappeared. Ul. Mostowa, running towards the southeast from the market in the direction of the Vistula River, laid out in the 19th century, led to the no longer existing Podgórski Bridge (only its pillars have been preserved – see p. 95), officially called the Franz Joseph Bridge.

In the northern part of the market square there is a magnificent Renaissance **TOWN HALL** 1. It has existed since the time of the town's foundation, although it is difficult to describe what it looked like then. It was rebuilt after the fire of 1557, when the tower topped by a bell-like cupola was added – one of the characteristic symbols of Kazimierz. Under the cupola there is a well-preserved bell, founded by town councillors in 1620. After the fire of 1623 the town hall received its visible Renaissance character, and has remained the same until the present day. In fact, apart from the Old Synagogue, the town hall is the only building in Kazimierz that has retained a magnificent Renaissance attic with blind arcades. Its present appearance is the result of thorough renovation conducted between 1875 and 1877. The level of the square was raised by 1.2 m, which greatly reduced its majestic character. Initially it was the Kazimierz councillors' office, an administrative-financial-judicial centre. Inside there were a courtroom, chancery, archives, hearing room, torture room and prison. After Kazimierz was annexed to Kraków, the town hall lost its significance and in 1830 it was turned into a Jewish school, which can be considered another symbol of Jewish-Christian coexistence in Kazimierz. As of 1870 Polish was the official language of instruction (including religious studies). The school was rather popular among the Reform Jews, and among its prominent graduates one may mention J. Oettingera and Jonathan Warszauer. Since 1949 the town hall has hosted the Seweryn Udziela Ethnography Museum (established in 1911), in possession of the wealthiest ethnographic collection in Poland, which in 2001 celebrated its 90th anniversary (see Practical Information). In the town hall's eastern wall we can see a copy (original in the National Museum, Warsaw) of the bas-relief by Henryk Hochman, depicting *Casimir the Great Greeting the Jews* (see p. 10).

We pass by a small fountain depicting *Three Musicians* by Bronisław Chromy. We head for the northeastern corner, where the massive

CORPUS CHRISTI CHURCH 2 [Kościół Bożego Ciała] is located with its 70-metre-tall tower – the most characteristic feature of the town, visible in old prints with a panoramic view of Kazimierz. The church was founded about 1340, but the building itself was completed in 1405. It was then that King Wladyslaw Jagiello brought the Canons Regular of Saint Augustine to Kraków, who in 1412 took over the parish and have been ministering to it until the present day. The monks supervised other building works that finally came to an end in 1477. In the early 17th century, the vigorous parish priest, Rev. Marcin Kłoczyński, who was in charge of the order from 1612 to 1644, introduced many embellishments. He added the tower with its outstanding manneristic copula, as well as three church porches on the western, northern and southern sides, topped by copulas and lanterns, built around stunning Gothic portals dating from 1405, canon's stalls and the main altar. During the Swedish invasion, the church was completely plundered and turned into storage rooms and stables. The Austrians and Russians also raided the church in the late 18th century; it has also suffered from several fires. Town councillors and wealthy burghers used to come to pray here, and together with the clergy they endowed the church generously.

It was at this church that an annual Corpus Christi procession was held. In one word – as one of the sermons preserved in the monastery archives says – "what the heart is for the living, the Corpus Christi Church is for Kazimierz". From the 15th century the church boasted a parish school, which was initially located at ul. Józefa 11 but then transferred to the newly erected building at ul. Bożego Ciała 24 (the building visible from the northern part of the courtyard).

The Gothic three-aisled building, ending with a long chancel, is surrounded by a complex of historical monuments belonging to the 16th-century monastery. The graveyard surrounding the church was enclosed by a tall wall and two gates from ul. św. Wawrzyńca and ul. Bożego Ciała. The cemetery was closed down in the late 18th century. At the foot of the bell tower, which contains four bells, we can see the mid-17th-century Gethsemane with sculptures of Jesus, the Virgin Mary and the Apostles. The top of the magnificent western façade, completed in 1477, is topped by pinnacles and ornamented by bas-reliefs of Christ, Saint Mary, St John the Apostle and the two emblems of Poland and Lithuania. We head for the main entrance below. On both sides of the entrance we can notice the small windows of the former church prison,

The magnificent facade of the Corpus Christi Church

where both men and women who had sinned against the sixth commandment were locked in; women for quarrelling and men for drinking too much. In the old days people leading promiscuous or disgraceful lives used to be exposed here to public mockery. We enter the church through the western porch and a beautiful Gothic portal. What attracts our attention is an unusual boat-shaped ambo with fishing-nets, oars, a mast and sails, floating on sea waves and supported by two mermaids. Its original shape can be explained by the verse placed beneath: *ascendens in naviculam Petri decebat turbas*, ('having entered the boat, Peter preached to the masses'), which is the essence of the apostolic mission of the Augustinian Canons. In the rood-screen at the entrance to the chancel we can see the 18th-century Christ on the Cross with His Mother, John the Apostle and kneeling Saint Mary Magdalene. The richly gilt main altar from 1634 features two paintings attributed to Tomasso Dolabella depicting *The Nativity* in the lower part, and *The Deposition of Christ* in the upper part; the whole altar is magnificent example of 17th-century woodcarving. The most outstanding works of art are the early Baroque canons' stalls placed along both sides of the chancel. On the southern wall we can admire 14th-century stained

glass windows. Behind the sacristy there is a treasure house where a 15th-century painting, *Madonna terribilis daemonibus*, is kept. The painting has been used since the Middle Ages as a means of exorcism – the process of expelling an evil spirit from a human body (hence its Latin name). This miraculous work of art is said to have scared away a hundred thousand demons, and is supposedly still used in the present day. We leave the chancel and on the right we can see the shrine of the beatified Stanisław Kazimierczyk, whose holy life ended in 1489. Opposite the shrine, in the left aisle we can see some other paintings by the renowned Tomasso Dolabella. We walk along the left aisle, and reach the Annunciation Chapel, mentioned in 1410. The present chapel dates from 1651 and hosts an early 16th-century painting of the Madonna, and a bronze font. Next to it there is St Ann's Chapel, founded in the early 15th century. The Brotherhood of the Most Holy Sacrament, active since 1346, is in charge of this chapel. In the early 17th century 'Five Wounds of Christ' was added to the Brotherhood's official name, and up to the present day the Brothers have ceremoniously participated in all church ceremonies, especially in Corpus Christi processions. Apart from a gilt painting of St Ann (16th cent.), there is the epitaph of Bartolomeo Berrecci, the renowned artist who designed the Sigismund Chapel in Wawel Cathedral. We can also notice two historical chests of drawers (1635). At the back of the church there is a Baroque choir supported by six pillars with a contemporary organ. In front of us is the Chapel of Our Lady of Częstochowa, originally from the mid-15th century; the present one, however, dates from the 1960s, when Poland celebrated the 1,000th anniversary of its baptism.

We leave the church through the northern porch and enter the former churchyard to cast a glance at the oldest wing of the monastery (15th c., adjoined with the church by a lovely passage supported by arcades), which is not accessible to the public.

We leave the former churchyard, and on the right we pass the former parish school. We turn right and reach the crossroads of ul. Bożego Ciała and ul. Józefa. We turn left and stop in front of the so-called **VOIVODE'S MANSION** 3, on the corner of Józefa and Krakowska Streets, on our right. It was here that Emperor Franz Joseph stayed in 1773 (see p. 20), in remembrance of which ul. Józefa (formerly known as Jewish Street) gained its present name. We cross ul. Krakowska; on the right at no. 13 we can see a grand palace-like mansion, known as **WOLF'S MANSION** 4, which consists of two mediaeval mansions joined into one for A. Wolf. This is where the famous Thorn Restaurant

was located; it served delicious Jewish meals: stuffed goose necks, pike with filling and Passover slivovitz.

We enter a narrow street, ul. św. Katarzyny, then we turn right into ul. Augustiańska (on the left we can see a 14th-century city wall turret that has been incorporated into the monastery complex), and then into ul. Paulińska. At the end of the street, on the left, there is a small gateway leading to the courtyard of the **ST MICHAEL THE ARCHANGEL AND ST STANISLAUS THE BISHOP MARTYR CHURCH** 5, popularly known as the (Pauline) Church On Skałka [the Rock]. As has already been mentioned, this church is traditionally associated with the death of Bishop Stanislaus of Szczepanów, who came into conflict with King

Boleslaw the Bold and is believed to have been murdered at the altar and then quartered. Until the present day the origins of the conflict are not entirely clear – an account made by a contemporary chronicler provides very little information. The detailed account by Bishop Wincenty Kadłubek, written a hundred years later, provided a basis for the canonisation process which was completed in 1253. Saint Stanislaus, whose martyrdom resembles St Thomas à Becket's murder in Canterbury Cathedral, was declared the main patron saint of Poland. We may recall that the

The lovely Baroque iron gate leading to the Church On Skałka

oldest settlement in Kazimierz was situated here on Skałka, with "a white stone church … where the Poles used to worship their pagan gods before they converted to Christianity" (Długosz). Soon Skałka had become the place of worship of St Stanislaus, and hundreds of people made pilgrimages here. King Casimir the Great erected a Gothic church here, and Jan Długosz brought the Pauline Order (Friars of Saint Paul the Hermit) to be in charge of Skałka.

An extremely ceremonious procession is associated with Skałka and the cult of St Stanislaus. Every year, on the first Sunday after 8th May (St Stanislaus Day), a procession with the saint's relics sets off from Wawel Cathedral. This picturesque procession is attended by nearly all Kraków clergy and townspeople. In the Skałka monastery courtyard we can see a pond, known, even in pagan times, for its curative qualities, which were later ascribed to St Stanislaus. In the 17th century the ornamented portal leading to the pond was added, as well as the pillars with four legendary eagles once guarding the corpse of St Stanislaus, whose stone figure can be seen in the middle of the pond accompanied by the knight, Piotrowin, believed to have been raised from the dead by the bishop. According to legend, when the bishop's body was being quartered, one of his fingers fell into the pond, a fish swallowed it and was miraculously caught afterwards. Some claimed that it was the bishop's head that had fallen into the pond and that this was why the water has a curative impact on eye and skin dysfunctions. Before we enter the church, we need to become aware of its historical significance. Starting in the 14th century, all Polish kings made a penitential pilgrimage on foot from Wawel to Skałka to expiate the deed of Boleslaw the Bold before their coronation. This act distinguished the church from all other churches in Poland. Thus, entering the church we shall remember that we are retracing the penitential path of Polish kings. Massive stairs lead through a late Baroque portal in the two-towered façade to the church, facing westward, unlike other Kazimierz churches and synagogues, which all face eastward. The three-aisled basilica is uniquely uniform in style – Baroque, with ornamented ceilings. The magnificent altar accommodates an 18th-century painting of St Michael the Archangel, the patron saint of the church. The altar in the north aisle on the right of the chancel, dating from 1745, made of black Dębnica marble, is even more important than the main altar. It is believed that the altar was erected on the spot where St Stanislaus was murdered on 11th April, 1079. The altar houses a painting of the saint in gilt vestments depicting 13th-century Skałka, and four eagles. The lower part of the altar contains a rather unusual object, namely a part of the tree trunk on which the bishop's body was chopped into pieces. What is more, a bit further to the right you can vaguely see, through three round holes, a stone splashed with the blood of the martyr (!), which is confirmed by a Latin inscription saying: "Stop, passerby, the Holy Bishop splashed me with his blood". We leave the church and go down to the Crypt of Honour [Krypta Zasłużonych] in the lower level of the church, a place especially important to Poles, where people who contributed greatly to Polish culture are buried. The crypt was established in 1880 when Jan Długosz (1415-80), prominent historian, chronicler and tutor of royal sons, was entombed for the second time on the 400th anniversary of his death. Soon the ashes of Lucjan Siemieński (1807-77), poet, prose writer and translator of eastern literature, were brought here; as well as those of Wincent Pol (1807-72), poet, geographer, and university professor. In 1887 the distinguished historical writer Józef Ignacy Kraszewski (1812-87) was buried here. His prolific output numbers 223 novels, and is unique in Polish and world literature. Other respected citizens include: Teofil Lenartowicz

(1822-93), one of the greatest 19th-century poets; Adam Asnyk (1838-97), poet and independence activist who combined positivist ideas with romanticism; Henryk Siemiradzki (1843-1902), poet and academic painter, whose canvas *Nero's Torches* served as the starting point for the National Museum in Kraków; Stanisław Wyspiański (1869-1907), one of Poland's greatest poets, playwrights, painters, graphic and stained glass designers, in love with Kraków throughout his life; Jacek Malczewski (1854-1929), outstanding allegorical and symbolic painter, and student of Jan Matejko; Karol Szymanowski (1882-1937), prominent Polish composer; Ludwik Solski (1855-1954), great actor, director and manager of the Juliusz Słowacki Theatre; and Tadeusz Banachiewicz (1882-1954), astronomer and mathematician. Thus, Skałka constitutes a National Pantheon, whose door is still open for other respected figures.

We leave this historic and nearly exclusively Baroque monument of Kazimierz through a lovely Baroque iron gate wrought in 1894 and displayed at the national exhibition in Lvov in the same year, evoking sensational reactions. In front of us is a picturesque passageway above ul. Skałeczna, joining the Augustinian Convent with the so-called Hungarian Chapel of St Catherine's Church, erected in 1728. There is a similar passageway at the Corpus Christi Church. We follow the monastery walls, passing the modern building of the Pauline Lower Secondary School (1935) and the Augustinian Convent. At the end of the street, on the left, we can see a small, separate building with a wooden roof – a 15th-century belfry. We stop in front of the massive **ST CATHERINE AND ST MARGARET'S CHURCH** 6 , founded by Casimir the Great, a fine example of Gothic architecture. As legend has it, the church was raised due to the king's infamous deed connected with the priest Marcin Baryczka. Although he was a great monarch, Casimir the Great had a guilty conscience about all the female hearts he had broken. Some chroniclers state that Baryczka had the courage to criticise the king's promiscuous life, which awakened the king's fury and led him to have the inconvenient priest drowned in the Vistula. King Casimir the Great had more wits about him than King Boleslaw the Bold, especially because Casimir was aware of the repercussions of his predecessor's deed, who met his poor end and was later considered a brutal and profane murderer. So, Casimir was more discreet, and in order to redeem his disgraceful deed, he immediately erected a few churches. First, he founded St Catherine and St Margaret's Church on the spot where Baryczka's body was found, and brought the Augustinian Hermits to look after it. Baryczka died in 1349, whereas the Augustinian friars had already been in Kraków since 1343, but it seems to make no difference for the legend, and King Casimir the Great is well-remembered and considered one of the greatest Polish monarchs we have ever had.

The church's history was not very fortunate – it was erected very quickly, begun in 1343 and completed in the late 14th century. The initial plans were altered for unknown reasons, and the church is 12.5 m shorter than originally planned, the façade has never been completed, nor the towers erected. In the earthquake of 1443 the ceiling collapsed. The flood of 1534 caused great damage to the church, as well as the fire of 1556 when the ceiling collapsed again and destroyed the main Gothic altar. Thomas de Robore, involved in renovations, died on the building site and his work was completed by Alexander Gucci and Antonio Morosi. In 1631 the church was renovated again, only to be turned into a military hospital, arsenal and stable 20 years later by the Swedes. Another earthquake, in 1786, caused the ceilings to crack, and the church was closed for safety reasons and the services were held in the cloisters. In 1796 the Austrian authorities ordered the church to be closed down, and the Baroque altars were destroyed. Although the Augustinians retrieved the church in 1814, its physical state had deteriorated so much that the town authorities decided

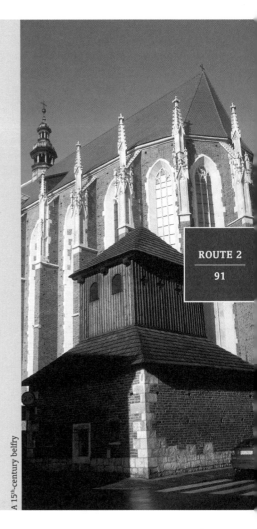

A 15th-century belfry

to demolish it. Fortunately, this never happened, and the church restoration was conducted by prominent architects from 1864 to World War I. The dissolution of the Augustinian Order in 1950 resulted in the negligence of the church. The Greek Orthodox were in charge of one of the chapels (St Dorothy) until 1998. The Augustinian Order, reactivated in 1989, has been in charge of the church and the monastery ever since. In 2002 they were awarded the title of 'Patron of Culture and the Arts in Kraków' for restoring the buildings to their former glory in the 1990s.

We enter the church through the southern porch and find ourselves in a magnificent, austere, three-aisled Gothic basilica. What is astonishing is that in the western wall there is a façade with a large, arched window, but no door – another example of the architectural mess when the church was built. On the right, in the southern wall, we can see the manneristic tomb of Wawrzyniec Spytek Jordan (died 1586), designed under the clear influence of Santi Gucci. Next to it is the slender figure of St Rita de Cascia, sculpted during World War II. She is the patron saint of difficult matters, wives and mothers. In the rood screen there is a 17th-century cross surrounded, rather unusually, by a group of angels holding the tools of the Passion, made during World War II. The chancel hosts a magnificent three-storey Baroque altar

from the 17th century, featuring the paintings *The Mystical Marriage of St Catherine* (1674) and *Eleven Beatified Martyrs of the Augustinian Order* (1869). In addition, the altar is ornamented by prominent Augustinian saints; the largest ones, on either side of the main painting, are St Augustine and St Thomas. A side doorway on the left leads us from the chancel into the cloister, and on our left we pass the sacristy. We are in a magnificent Gothic monastic cloister with recently renovated frescos on the walls. We turn left and pass through the Chapel of the Beatified Izajasz Boner (died 1471), founded in 1776, containing the Kazimierz saint's relics. Behind the grill there is the Chapel of Our Consoling Lady, separated from the cloister before 1436, with a magnificent mural dating from the early 15th century depicting Madonna and child (1504-1512), recently embellished with golden crowns. We can walk along the cloister, and we pass St Dorothy's Chapel, erected before 1365, with a splendid mural depicting *St Augustine Establishing his Order* (1425). Above the side entrance there is a 15th-century image of *Christ and Misericordia Domini* [The Suffering Mother]. On the northern wall (to the right of the entrance) we can see 15th-century murals depicting St Augustine and scenes from the martyrdom of St Catherine and Margaret, as well as the *Scala Peccatorum* – an interesting scene of man's death with Satan and an angel fighting for his soul. On our way we pass the tomb of an unknown knight, attributed to Santi Gucci. We are back in the northern aisle, with Baroque paintings dating from the early 17th century depicting the miracles performed by St Augustine. Heading towards the exit, on our right we can see the aforementioned Hungarian Chapel (St Monica's Chapel), founded in the early 15th century. Since 1727 the chapel has belonged to the Augustinian Nuns, who established their oratory here. The chapel is inaccessible to the public all year except for 26th April – the day of Our Lady of Good Advice – the only opportunity to enter the chapel. It is to access this chapel that the nuns use the narrow passageway above ul. Skałeczna.

We reach the corner where ul. Skałeczna crosses ul. Krakowska, and on the right-hand corner we can see the **NUREMBERG HOUSE** 7 opened in 1996 after a thorough renovation of the Gothic mansion, a counterpart to the Kraków House in Nuremberg. It houses the Nuremberg Restaurant and a conference room which hosts many cultural events.

We turn right, walk along ul. Krakowska, and pass the town hall, now seen from a different angle. On the left at no. 46 there is **ESTERKA'S HOUSE** 8, the house of the aforementioned legendary mistress of King Casimir, whose charm and beauty captured his heart. In the 16th century the renowned Renaissance architect Bartolomeo

Legend of Esterka

It was believed that it was King Casimir's love for the beautiful Jewess, Esterka, that influenced the privileges he granted Jews (apparently Esterka lived in a house at ul. Krakowska 46, although there are many (houses of Esterka) in Kraków). Casimir's beloved Esterka gave birth to the king's two daughters and two sons, who unfortunately could not pass as official offspring, since they were born out of wedlock. Esterka was introduced to history by Jan Długosz, who justified King Casimir's friendly attitude towards Jews by this relationship. However, other sources, especially that written by Janko of Czarnków, contemporary to King Casimir, do not mention her; so this story, then, may be considered a contrived romance which had a great impact on perception of Christian-Jewish relations. "The king's recognition of Esterka's beauty – both physical and moral – and his subsequent desire to procreate with her – is read by Jews as an invitation to participate as full partners in the Polish nation ... However, what are we to make of the fact that the very myth of the Polish-Jewish symbiosis is constructed on an unequal power relationship, on marital and national betrayals, and on forbidden love?"

Prof. Justin Cammy in his lecture on Yiddish literature (Jagiellonian University, 2002)

Berecci lived here. Following a thorough renovation in the 1970s and 1980s, the house became a host of the Ethnography Museum. We cross ul. Skawińska, at the end of which the above-mentioned St Jacob's Church once stood.

On the right, at ul. Krakowska 43, the Brother Albert historical shelter house was located (see pp. 25, 26). Nowadays, the order's head office is located here together with the small **BROTHER ALBERT'S MUSEUM** 9, containing a collection of personal items and his paintings. The classical façade features a plaque commemorating Brother Albert and his canonisation in 1989. We cross the street, pass the Hospitaller Brothers' Monastery erected between 1741 and 1751, and head for the most beautiful façade in Kraków – if not in Poland – the late Baroque **CHURCH OF THE MOST HOLY TRINITY** 10, designed by Francis Placidi. It initially belonged to the Trinitarians, but since 1812 it has belonged to the Hospitaller Brothers. In the mid-18th century an outstanding late Baroque church was erected in the style of Francesco Borromini: restless and picturesque, and at the same time sophisticated and reserved. In the late 19th century and again in the 1960s the church was renovated. We enter the one-naved church, surrounded by narrow chapels and with a ceiling dissolved in beautiful painted scenes depicting *The Redemption of Christian Slaves from Muslim Captivity by St John of Matha*, founder of the Trinitarians. Nearby,

in ul. Trynitarska, stands the **HOSPITALLER BROTHERS' HOSPITAL** 11, erected between 1897 and 1906 on the 50th anniversary of Emperor Franz Joseph's rule. The building was designed by the prominent Kraków architect Teodor Talowski. On the façade we can see the emblems of the Austro-Hungarian Empire, Poland, Kraków and the Hospitaller Brothers, as well as the figure of St John of God, founder of the Hospitaller Brothers. Having left the Church of the Most Holy Trinity, we head for the bridge, one of the most characteristic sights of Kazimierz. On the way, on the right we can see some remnants of the city walls. We enter the picturesque **MARSHAL JÓZEF PIŁSUDSKI BRIDGE** 12, the so-called Second Bridge across the Vistula, erected between 1925 and 1933 in order to replace the heavily exploited Podgórski Bridge. The bridge's span is 72 m long. Partly destroyed in 1945, it was restored in 1948. Several metres towards the east there was the former Podgórski Bridge, erected between 1844 and 1850, officially called the Emperor Franz Joseph Bridge, although the name was never used. If we look towards ul. Mostowa in Kazimierz, and ul. Brodzińskiego on the other bank, we can see the stone pillars that once supported the bridge. We gaze back at Christian Gothic-Baroque Kazimierz and end our tour. Now we can follow Route 3, or just walk along the Vistula.

The picturesque Marshal Piłsudski Bridge

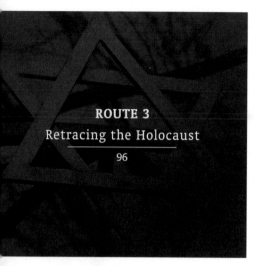

1 the Isaac Synagogue
2 Transitory camp
3 Jewish Fighting Organisation (ŻOB) Headquarters
4 Gate I
5 Isolation Hospital
6 the Pharmacy Under the Eagle – National Remembrance Museum
7 Optical Glass-Works
8 Szymon Lustgarten's house
9 Jewish Social Self-Help Office
10 Jewish Hospital
11 Ward for the Chronically Ill
12 Main Gate (II)
13 Jewish Council (*Judenrat*)
14 Madritsch Factory
15 Roman Polański's house
16 the Zucher Synagogue
17 Optima Factory
18 Old People's Home
19 Orphanage
20 Isolation Hospital
21 Regional Court
22 Gate III
23 Fragment of the Ghetto Wall
24 Gate IV
25 Fragment of the Ghetto Wall
26 the Płaszów Camp
27 Ruins of the former Funeral House
28 Podgórski Cemetery (former)
29 'Grey House'
30 Camp Commander Amon Goeth's Villa
31 Monument Commemorating the First German Execution
32 Roll-Call Square
33 Monument Commemorating the Unknown Jews
34 Monument Commemorating the Hungarian Jewesses
35 Monument Commemorating the Martyrs

This route takes about 3 hours, and will lead you through places that witnessed the most terrifying moments in Jewish history and in the history of Kraków. For many people, especially those who have roots in Kraków, this will be a deeply emotional experience. And for others, especially the younger generation – it will be a live history lesson about something which should not be forgotten, so that such a tragedy will never happen again.

OPTION I ul. Kupa > ul. Józefa > ul. Wąska > ul. św. Wawrzyńca > ul. Starowiślna > Powstańców Śląskich Bridge

OPTION II Plac Bohaterów Getta > ul. Targowa > ul. Węgierska > ul. Limanowskiego > Rynek Podgórski > ul. Rękawka > ul. Węgierska > ul. Limanowskiego > ul. Krakusa > ul. Rękawka > ul. Czarnieckiego > ul. Józefińska > ul. Lwowska > ul. Limanowskiego > ul. Wielicka > ul. Jerozolimska > ul. Hetmana > ul. Abrahama

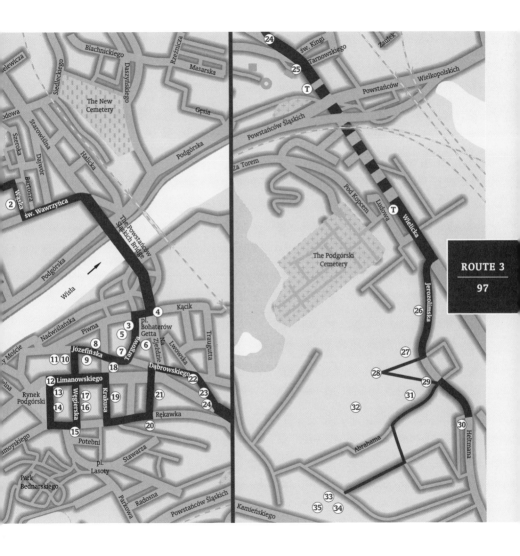

Before commencing the tour, it is recommended to go back to Chapter 1 and refer to the Holocaust history brief. There are two optional beginnings of the tour: those who have more time at their disposal (and have not yet visited Jewish Kazimierz) can start at the Isaac Synagogue (option I), while those who do not have much time, or have already visited Jewish Kazimierz or the Isaac Synagogue, can start at Bohaterów Getta Square (option II).

OPTION I: We start at the **ISAAC SYNAGOGUE** 1 (see p. 70), where war-time films are shown. We definitely should watch the short film made in 1941 *The Removal to the Cracow Ghetto* (shot by the Germans), showing the exodus of the Jewish population to a suburb which later became a 'porch of hell'. The film enables us to travel back in time and see with our own eyes people wearing armbands marked with the Star of David, separate tram compartments for Jews and non-Jews (*für Juden, nicht-Juden*), and above all anxious and miserable people uncertain of their fate, carrying their belongings to the other bank of the Vistula River to a suburb called Podgórze – the authentic inhabitants of Kazimierz. From the synagogue we walk along ul. Kupa until we reach ul. Józefa, then we turn left, pass ul. Jakuba (where the main gate to the Jewish town was once located), and reach ul. Wąska. There – in a magnificent building on the right (now a secondary school), the **TRANSITORY CAMP** 2 was located between 1939 and 1945, as the plaque next to the entrance informs us. People captured during a so-called 'raid' were brought here before they were transferred to concentration or death camps. We turn left into ul. św. Wawrzyńca, reach ul. Starowiślna, turn right and cross the Powstańców Śląskich Bridge. From here we have a beautiful view of the Marshal Józef Piłsudski Bridge with its characteristic span, which we have already seen in the 1941 film shown at the Isaac Synagogue – Jews crossed it while moving to Podgórze. On the right we can see a panoramic view of Kazimierz spreading between the two bridges and on the left a panoramic view of the former ghetto in Podgórze with the Vistula River as a border between these two entirely different worlds. Leaving the bridge behind, we enter the area of the former ghetto, centred around Bohaterów Getta Square and Limanowskiego and Józefińska Streets.

OPTION II: We are at Plac Bohaterów Getta [Heroes of the Ghetto] Square (formerly known as Plac Zgody [Agreement Square]), located in the northern part of the ghetto. In the years 1941-43 this was the so-called

Umschlagplatz, the square where Jews had to gather before they were transferred to the Bełżec death camp (June and October 1942). During the liquidation action in 1943, on 13th March, people were marched to the Płaszów Camp from here, and on 14th March hundreds of elderly Ghetto B inmates were shot in the square and its vicinity: in ul. Piwna women were executed and in the nearby ul. Nadwiślańska – children left in the Children's Home (*Kinderheim*). The square also witnessed the tragic events of 'Bloody Thursday' – 4th June, 1942 when the prominent Yiddish poet Mordechai Gebirtig (see box p. 76) was murdered together with his family and other distinguished figures of the ghetto. On that day there were numerous other bestial manslaughters, and terrible suffering of people separated from their families, uncertain of the following day, if not the next hour. The western side of the square (buildings at nos. 2-5) on the right side of the bridge has not changed since the war. The building at no. 6 housed the **JEWISH FIGHTING ORGANISATION (ŻOB) HEADQUARTERS 3**. The plaque reads: "To commemorate the heroes and martyrs of the Kraków Ghetto murdered by the German barbarians. This building housed the Jewish Fighting Organisation Headquarters". This plaque was made on the fifth anniversary of the ghetto liquidation on 13th March 1948 by the citizens' committee. The young ghetto fighters who met here (see p. 35) were involved in sabotage activity, and launched a rather successful attack on the German café, Cyganeria, in ul. Szpitalna in December of 1942. On the other side of the square we can see a narrow street, ul. Kącik: between the building at no. 2 and a non-existing building at Plac Zgody 10, **GATE I 4** leading to the ghetto was situated. It was mainly the pedestrian gate, through which most food was smuggled into the ghetto, since it was the least guarded gate. We head towards ul. Targowa, where on the right, in the backyard of the building at Plac Bohaterów Getta 3, after the June resettlement action the **ISOLATION HOSPITAL 5** was located, which had been moved from its original location at ul. Rękawka 30 (see p. 107). During the ghetto liquidation all the hospital inmates were shot – in the façade of the preserved building we can still see bullet holes. The staff of this hospital, like the staff of other hospitals, were transferred to the Płaszów Camp.

At the corner of ul. Targowa and Plac Bohaterów Getta, at no. 18, there is the former **PHARMACY 'UNDER THE EAGLE' 6** in 1983 turned into the **NATIONAL REMEMBRANCE MUSEUM**. The owner of the pharmacy, Tadeusz Pankiewicz (1908-93), was the only gentile inhabitant of the ghetto. The Germans, fearing the outbreak of a typhoid epidemic, consented to the pharmacy's existence, which was open 24 hours, 7 days a week, as of October 1941, and was the only place where a patch of the previous free world had been preserved. "The pharmacy was, in the opinion of most of the people, a sort of embassy, a diplomatic station, representing the world, singularly free, within the walled and imprisoned city. It became a daily meeting place for many interesting people. Here, one could find assembled at certain hours of the day, people of all ages and in all walks of life. Here, from early morning the German newspapers and underground press were read, the latest war communiqués could be studied and commented upon, and the political situation assessed. Here, also, the daily problems and worries were discussed. Conversations continuing far into the night weighed the future prognostications" (T. Pankiewicz, *The Cracow Ghetto Pharmacy*). It was here that scientists, artists, doctors, lawyers, writers or journalists met; among others Abraham Neumann, a gifted painter, or the above-mentioned Mordechai Gebirtig. Pankiewicz used to be visited by Jews working for the Germans, as well as "German police patrols, composed mostly of Viennese,

... I have to admit that the visiting policemen (Viennese) behaved quite correctly to the Jews met there; they always addressed them as 'Mr.' and spoke with them as if they never heard of discrimination". The pharmacy's location allowed the observation of a large space, since its windows overlooked Plac Zgody and ul. Targowa, so Tadeusz Pankiewicz and his staff witnessed the cruelest atrocities committed by the Nazis. Pankiewicz wrote a shocking account called *The Cracow Ghetto Pharmacy* (first published in 1947; other editions followed in 1983, 1995 and 2003), thanks to which we can learn about individual stories of ghetto inmates, the ghetto atmosphere, and see the deportation or liquidation actions through the eyes of one of the ghetto inhabitants, which is extremely valuable, for – according to Raphael Scharf – "historical events become close and more real when perceived through individual people's experience". Apart from Tadeusz Pankiewicz, the pharmacy's staff included three ladies: Irena Droździkowska, Helena Krywaniuk and Aurelia Danek-Czortowa, who were engaged in helping Jews from the beginning of the ghetto's existence; since they did not possess permission to stay in the ghetto, they soon became intermediaries between the ghetto inmates, cut off from the outside world, and people living outside the ghetto. As Tadeusz Pankiewicz recalls: "They took care of applications, delivered correspondence, became intermediaries in various affairs between Polish acquaintances living outside the Ghetto and the Jews, purchased food, … They also provided difficult-to-obtain medications … and brought in small [valuable] objects [and money] hidden with the Polish people by Jews when they left Cracow to live in the Ghetto. … It was well known that this kind of help, transferring scrip or valuable objects, was quite dangerous". Both the pharmacy owner and his staff helped many inhabitants of the ghetto by giving them medicines free of charge, when they could not afford them; helping them arrange false documents, which often made escape possible; and Tadeusz Pankiewicz himself often offered nightly shelter in the pharmacy for those who were hunted for by the Germans or who wanted to avoid being resettled. In 1983 Tadeusz Pankiewicz was awarded the medal of the 'Righteous Among the Nations', he lived in Kraków till the end of his days and was buried at Rakowicki Cemetery.

The National Remembrance Museum, hosted by the former pharmacy, provides us with an opportunity to learn more about the wartime history of the Kraków Jews and see original photographs from the ghetto and Płaszów Camp. We can also see a list of ŻOB members,

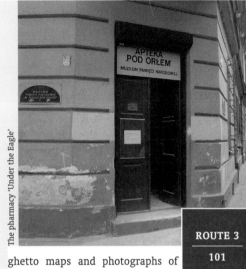

The pharmacy 'Under the Eagle'

ghetto maps and photographs of Nazi executioners. One room is devoted to Tadeusz Pankiewicz; we can see the pharmacy furniture, his photographs, and – what is perhaps the most touching in this part of the museum – his original writing desk (on the left), with letters of gratitude from all over the world. As Pankiewicz recalls: "I must say, without exaggeration, that we were well liked by everybody, and that during the entire time of our Ghetto existence, we did not have a single argument, unpleasantness, or trouble with the Ghetto inhabitants. We were met at every step with signs of overwhelming and perhaps even unjustified gratitude. Many letters from camps and, after liberation, from different countries of Europe, came and continued to come to prove that the ties of empathy knotted during the common life in the Ghetto were permanent". Having left the museum, we turn left and walk along ul. Targowa, which became the border between Ghetto A and B after the October 1942 deportation (see p. 31). Let us recall that Ghetto A – on the right – was inhabited by the employed, whereas Ghetto B – by the unemployed, elderly and ill.

On the right, at ul. Targowa 6, (the original building no longer exists, now a dwelling house at no. 4) there was Feliks Dziuba's **OPTICAL GLASS-WORKS** 7. He and his three employees had permanent passes and were also involved in smuggling food and medicine into the ghetto. In the June deportation of 1942 Feliks Dziuba obtained 20 *blauschein*, blue cards – permission to stay in the ghetto, and fictitiously hired 20 Jews in his factory, saving them from death. We turn right into one of the two main streets of the ghetto – ul. Józefińska. The ŻOB members used to meet in the building at no. 13, in **SZYMON LUSTGARTEN'S HOUSE** 8. "They [members of the Jewish Fighting Organisation ŻOB] rejected the concept of the Jewish Council that work performed perfectly and absolute obedience im-

proved chances of survival. ... Fully aware that the Germans aimed at the total annihilation of the Jews, they appealed to the boycotting of German regulations, sabotage and active resistance against the occupant's violence. ... The youth of this organisation had chosen the fate of an unequal and tough fight against the invader, aware – as Liebeskind used to say – that 'there is no return from this path. We tread a path of death ... Who desires life, shall not search for it among us. We are at our end. But our end is not twilight. Our end is death, which a strong man chooses to meet." The organisation was headed by the aforementioned Adolf Liebeskind, Abraham Lejbowicz and Szymon Dränger. Unfortunately, most of the ŻOB members were arrested after the attack at the Cyganeria Café on 22/24 December 1942.

The magnificent building on the left, at no. 18, housed the **JEWISH SOCIAL SELF-HELP OFFICE** 9, established immediately after the outbreak of the war. The organisation was presided over by a seven-person board chaired by Dr Michał Weichert. It received subventions from the American Jewish Joint Distribution Committee (known as 'Joint'), International Red Cross and charity organisations, thanks to which members of the Jewish Social Self-Help could distribute medicine, dressings, medical equipment

Michał Weichert (1890-1967), founder of the Warsaw Yiddish Theatre, member of the Vilno Troupe, theatrologist, during World War II presided over the Jewish Social Self-Help in Warsaw, then moved to the Kraków ghetto. As Tadeusz Pankiewicz recalls: "After March 1943 [after the ghetto liquidation] he skilfully organized, jointly with Dr Hilfstein, Dr Tisch, A. Bieberstein, S. Jaszczurka and Dr L. Leinkram, the distribution of medicine and food to the camp in Płaszów and all the others in Poland. After visiting the camps in Płaszów and all others in Cracow and its surroundings, he helped the inmates, groups or individuals at the risk of his own life. He carried correspondence and monies from the Poles for the Jews. ... [However] After Poland regained its independence, Dr Weichert was sued for not obeying the recommendation of the Jewish underground organization to cease his activities. ... In the court proceedings he maintained that he wished to remain in contact with the representative of the underground in order to present his position and to prove that he really helped the people interned in the camps. The organisation, however, disagreed with contentions and even issued an order for his liquidation, which did not take place. The trial proved conclusively that Dr Weichert could, with the help of Polish and Jewish organisations, have gone abroad or hidden in a monastery. But he never availed himself of these opportunities. He proved, without a doubt, that the assistance which he provided saved the lives of many people. A few years after the war, the Weicherts left Poland and settled in Israel, where the doctor was heartily welcomed by his former students and friends. ... He published three volumes of memoirs and a large volume devoted to the Jewish Social Self-Help organization". Regarded as a controversial figure by many people, he is nevertheless seen by those who lived contemporary with him as a person who did a lot of good supporting Jews in dramatically harsh conditions.

and food to the ghetto, the Camp in Płaszów and other institutions in the vicinity of Kraków. They were permitted to buy food at fixed prices (i.e. 15-20% of free market prices), which allowed them to support charity canteens, hospitals and other charity organisations. In 1942 the Germans dissolved JSSH, and established the *Jüdische* Unterstützung-Stelle [Aid Point for Jews, JUS] instead. Shortly before the ghetto liquidation, Michał Weichert handed over the vast majority of parcels to *Rada Główna Opiekuńcza* [Main Protective Council], thanks to which they were shipped to the camp in Brünnlitz, where the Schindler Jews had been transferred. JUS ultimately ceased to exist after the liquidation of the Płaszów camp in 1944.

A few steps away, the building at ul. Józefińska 14 hosted the **JEWISH HOSPITAL** 10 , transferred here from ul. Skawińska 8 in October of 1941 (see Route 1). Although modestly equipped, it provided excellent services due to extremely devoted doctors and medical personnel. The hospital had 120 beds, but was often so overcrowded that two patients lay in one bed. The director of the hospital was the prominent surgeon Dr Józef Nüssenfeld. It is worth mentioning that even in those dreadful times regular weekly scientific meetings were held. The most tragic day for the hospital was 28th October, when only doctors and medical personnel were excluded from deportation. Nevertheless, along with the patients unable to leave hospital, several doctors were deported and murdered. On the day of the ghetto liquidation most doctors and patients of the hospital were executed. It was here that Dr Rozalia Blau died because she did not want to leave her patient Dr Bergerowa behind. Dr Zygmunt Fischer and Dr Bruno Palin, along with their wives and children, encountered the same fate.

At the end of 1941, at ul. Józefińska 10, the **WARD FOR THE CHRONICALLY ILL** 11 of the Main Hospital was established with 50 beds, run by its founders: Dr Bernard Bornstein and Dr Julian Aleksandrowicz, prominent philanthropist, doctor and author of the memoirs *Kartki z dziennika doktora Twardego*. During the June 1942 deportation about 470 people found shelter in this hospital, and thanks to the doctors' cleverness, were saved. The hospital functioned till the ghetto liquidation in 1943. The same building also hosted the German labour department (*Arbeitsamt*), where all people forwarded to forced labour were listed, and lists of those to be deported were made. Initially the department was headed by a Viennese, K. Scheppessy, who issued dozens of fictitious work allocations; however, the Gestapo found out about it quickly and he was arrested and executed shortly afterwards. The *Arbeitsamt* was liquidated after the October 1942 deportation. We go back towards ul. Węgierska. The building at no. 16 hosted the Jewish Council Offices from June 1942. We turn right into ul. Limanowskiego. We reach the Podgórski Market Square, where the **MAIN GATE (II)** 12 to the ghetto was situated; it joined the building at Rynek Podgórski 15 with no. 1. It was both for pedestrians (the pavement near Rynek Podgórski 15) and the tram (no. 3), cars and carts. All those employed outside the ghetto walked in and out through this gate every day, as well as the pharmacy staff, court employees, and occasionally Polish doctors called for consultations by Jewish doctors. The gate had a semicircular topping in the form of Jewish tombstones and bore an inscription in Yiddish (written in the Hebrew alphabet): *Judischer Wohnbezirk* [Jewish District]. The gate was guarded by German and Polish policemen in navy blue uniforms, and one needed a special pass to get in, obtainable at the German Police Station at Rynek Podgórski 1. The corner building at ul. Limanowskiego 2, the former Podgórze town council, housed the **JEWISH COUNCIL OFFICE** 13 (*Judenrat*). "The work in the Judenrat was very hateful for conscientious people. It was not easy to carry out orders against one's will, to circumvent the law, to play for delays, to quietly and tactfully convince the multitude of people that the Judenrat did not issue any orders, but, under duress, merely obeyed the Germans' demands" – claims Tadeusz Pankiewicz. The Jewish Council had lost its religious character and had to face the incredibly difficult task of repelling and alleviating German orders, as well as organising labour and support for the poor and homeless. The first president of the Council, Prof. Marek Bieberstein – deeply involved in philanthropy before the war, a man with a heart of gold entirely devoted to people – aimed at the protection of Jews against the German invaders. In 1940, after the regulation on mass expulsion, according to which only 15,000 Jews were permitted to stay in Kraków, he paid a representative of the *Stadthauptmann*, Mr Reichert, a bribe of 100,000 zlotys, for which

the latter had pledged to issue permission to stay for another 10,000 people. Marek Bieberstein was denounced and received a two-year prison sentence, and then was sent to the Płaszów camp where he died in 1944. The succeeding president of the Council, Dr Artur Rosenzweig, "was a virtuous and respectable man who never served the Germans. He was forced to take that post and he found performing his duties burdensome and sorrowful. All the time he was apathetic and sad, he complained about his total impotence against the violence destroying all his intentions and efforts" – as Aleksander Bieberstein recalls. During the June deportation, Artur Rosenzweig was accused of faulty conduct and forced to join the group of displaced people, and together with his family was sent to Bełżec where he died in a gas chamber. The succeeding president, Dawid Gutter, by then referred to as a commissioner, who could not boast a high moral standard, eagerly fulfilled German orders, blindly believing in their victory and his survival. He was executed together with his family in the Płaszów Camp in 1944. The same fate was shared by the Council secretary, Dr Samuel Streimer, who, like Gutter, extremely eagerly obeyed Nazi orders and even tried to exceed them in cruelty. Only a few Council members survived the Holocaust. After the June deportation, the Council office was transferred to ul. Węgierska 16.

We are now at the west end of the ghetto, at Rynek Podgórski. The northern and eastern side of the square belonged to the ghetto, the southern side together with St Joseph's Church and the western side did not; ul. Limanowskiego, where we stand now, was the ghetto's main street, and after June 1942, when the area of the ghetto was reduced, it became its southern border. We walk along the eastern side of Rynek Podgórski towards the church. On the left we pass the aforementioned Jewish Council Office (now the Town Magistrate building), and the former German Police Station next to it. We stop at the building at Rynek Podgórski 3, where the **MADRITSCH FACTORY** 14 was located, named after its owner, Julius Madritsch, who displayed great generosity towards his Jewish employees. Moreover, he obtained additional work cards, which prevented people from being deported. The factory produced army garments; during the war the entrance to the factory led from ul. Węgierska 10. After the ghetto liquidation it continued to function, and then was transferred to a workshop in Płaszów.

We walk along the square and reach ul. Rękawka. Here, in the building at no. 2 was **ROMAN POLAŃSKI'S HOUSE** 15, where he lived, as a child, during the Second World War. We turn left into ul. Węgierska. On the right at no. 5 we can see the building of the former **ZUCHER SYN-AGOGUE** 16, erected between 1879 and 1881 by the former Jewish community in Podgórze. Nowadays, it houses one of the most remarkable contemporary art galleries – the Starmach Gallery. Next to it, at no. 7/9, we can see the entrance to the courtyard of the former **OPTIMA FACTORY** 17, situated between ul. Węgierska and parallel ul. Krakusa. The former chocolate factory housed, during the time of the ghetto, Jewish crafts workshops – mainly tailor, shoe, tanner, saddler and carpenter workshops that operated for *Zentrale für Handwerkslieferungen*. The courtyard witnessed the deportations of 1942 when hundreds of people were rounded up here on 6th June, 1942, kept for two hot days with no food, no lavatories, separated from their families, uncertain of what was to follow, only to be marched to the Prokocim railway station and sent to Bełżec. We walk along ul. Węgierska, and again reach ul. Limanowskiego, where at no. 15 there is the building of the former **OLD PEOPLE'S HOME FOR THE CHRONICALLY ILL** 18, founded by Dr Jakub Kranz. The home's inmates were over 70 years old or in need of constant care. During the June deportation many people were hidden here, as in the isolation hospital. However, during the October deportation the home was liquidated and all inmates unable to move were executed together with head of the home, Dr Jakub Kranz.

We return to ul. Krakusa, where, on the façade of the building at no. 7, we can still see the inscription OPTIMA, which reminds us of the factory and its history. On the left at no. 8 stands the building of the former Róża Rockowa **ORPHANAGE** 19. The commemorative plaques tell us about the donor, Amalja Wasserbergerowa. The orphanage was located here from May 1941 until June 1942. After the June deportation, ul. Krakusa was excluded from the ghetto and the orphanage was transferred to ul. Józefińska 31. In September 1942 it was moved again to a former kindergarten at ul. Józefińska 41, through the infamous efforts of the Jewish Police Head, Symche Spira, who adapted the building for the Jewish policemen. The orphanage was supported by the Jewish Social Self-Help, as well as the by Jewish Community, generous even in such extremely difficult times. The building, which no longer exists, witnessed the tragic end of the orphanage: on 28th October, 1942 the orphanage was liquidated: small children were driven outside town, while the older ones were gathered at Plac Zgody, from where they were marched to the Prokocim railway station with head of the orphanage, Anna Feuerstein, and her husband, who rejected the German offer to remain in the ghetto, together with Dawid Kurzmann, who had devoted his entire life to these children.

We return to ul. Rękawka. It is worth mentioning that this was the only green area in the ghetto until June 1942, when the ghetto territory was reduced; it served as a walking promenade and resting place. Here at no. 30 the **ISOLATION HOSPITAL** 20 was initially located. It was established by Aleksander Bieberstein, author of *Annihilation of the Jews in Kraków*. "The hospital was opened at the end of 1939 through the generosity of the whole community. The entire staff, both paid and volunteer, was characterised by extraordinary generosity, kindness and care for the patients' welfare; it was only thanks to them that running the hospital in such harsh conditions was possible" – recalls Aleksander Bieberstein. During the June deportation, from which patients were excluded, about 350 people hid in the hospital. After the reduction of the ghetto's territory, the hospital was transferred to the building at Plac Zgody 3 (see p. 99). During the October deportation, which included patients, the vast majority of mobile patients were hidden or released, and since the health personnel were excluded from the deportation, many patients were dressed as doctors. However, when the hospital was liquidated in March 1943, the patients were ordered to remain in the hospital, whereas the staff was transferred to the Płaszów camp.

We go down along ul. Czarnieckiego, and on the right, at no. 3, we pass the former building of the **REGIONAL COURT** 21, now a custody.

The fragment of the Ghetto wall

tablished here (see p. 32), for children whose parents worked. Children living here were executed in Zgody Square during the liquidation in March 1943. Ul. Józefińska 39 was where the Jewish Police Station was situated (*Ordnungsdienst*; see p. 29), whose members, 'OD-men', are remembered mostly for their infamous deeds: by their hand hundreds of people ended up in death camps. It is difficult to formulate their attitude; those who did not possess a great deal of character or lacked moral fibre often surrendered and blindly obeyed German orders, hoping to survive and protect their families. The Nazis quickly showed them they were wrong – the notorious head of the Jewish Police, Symche Spira, as well as the majority of his workers and their families, were executed in Płaszów in December 1943. We continue along ul. Józefińska and reach ul. Lwowska. Here the third **GATE (III)** 22 was located diagonally, through which all the deportees walked from Zgody Square to the Prokocim railway station, and then were sent to death camps, or, after the liquidation, to the Płaszów camp. In ul. Lwowska between the buildings at nos. 25-29 spreads one of the two preserved **FRAGMENTS OF THE GHETTO WALL** 23. The wall witnessed the everyday life, suffering and last moments of the ghetto inhabitants, who passed it on their last march towards Płaszów. The commemorative plaque says in Polish and Yiddish:

Barristers coming for trials here, among others Mieczysław Kossek, a school friend of Tadeusz Pankiewicz, issued fictitious warrants to the Civil Court which enabled a number of Jews to leave the ghetto. We cross ul. Limanowskiego, and reach ul. Józefińska again. During the rebuilding of the public transportation lines in Podgórze, the buildings at nos. 37-41 were demolished. On the opposite side we can see buildings which look as though they were sliced with a knife. At ul. Józefińska 41, as already mentioned, there stood an orphanage from September 1942 to its liquidation in October 1942; afterwards a Children's Home (*Kinderheim*) was es-

"This is where they lived, suffered and died at the hands of the Hitlerite executioners. This was their last walk to the death camps".

We reach ul. Limanowskiego again, where between the buildings at nos. 50 and 31, exactly at the pedestrian crossing, **GATE IV** 24 – only for mechanical vehicles or army troops – was located. We cross the street and head left for a school at ul. Limanowskiego 62. Behind the school on the right there stands the other **FRAGMENT OF THE GHETTO WALL** 25, recently renovated. The surroundings have changed a great deal since the wartime, the hill is now covered with trees and bushes, the level of the ground has also been raised, since the wall used to be much taller. Having left the school yard, we head for the former Płaszów Camp. We can get there on foot – it is about a 30-minute walk – or by any tram – one stop to Podgórski Cemetery, then we walk for a while and turn into ul. Jerozolimska, which leads to the former camp territory.

THE PŁASZÓW CAMP 26 (see p. 34) was established on the territory of two Jewish cemeteries: one belonged to the former Jewish Community in Podgórze and its entrance was situated at ul. Jerozolimska 25, and the other belonged to the Kraków Jewish Community, with its entrance at ul. Abrahama 3. Both covered an area of 10 hectares. During the camp's erection both cemeteries were destroyed, and the tombstones were used as building material for barracks and pavements. In the course of time, the camp was expanded south towards ul. Pańska; all the previous inhabitants were evicted and their houses were taken over by the SS-officers appointed to work in the camp. The camp spread west towards ul. Swoszowicka and east towards ul. Wielicka, and by 1944 it had grown to 80 hectares with dozens of barracks, both residential and 'industrial' ones, housing workshops where the camp inmates worked. Let us walk along one of the camp streets – ul. Jerozolimska. Before we reach the building on the right, we can turn right into a field path and after several metres of thick bushes we can just make out the **RUINS OF THE FORMER FUNERAL HOUSE** 27. The building was partly blown up in order to make space for an additional railway line. We walk on, and after about 100 m we reach a path crossing. We turn right and walk along a path going slightly up the hill, which leads to the former **PODGÓRSKI CEMETERY** 28 located on a small hill. We can find many tombs stripped of their tombstones, and the only tombstone of Chaim Jakub Abrahamer, who died in 1932 (with inscriptions in Polish and Hebrew). It has survived all the vicissitudes of history and stands here alone, reminding us of the Jewish cemetery that once existed here.

We return along the path towards the crossing with the narrow ul. Abrahama; in front of us on the right we can see the **'GREY HOUSE'** 29 at ul. Jerozolimska 3. The building used to belong to the Chewra Kadisha Funeral Society, and during World War II it was turned into the SS Headquarters and its cellars housed SS torture chambers. The cruelest SS officers lived here: "Hujar, Zdrojewski, Landsdorfer, Ekert and Glaser..., and the cellars housed a prison, not an ordinary prison but a genuine casemate of tortures. He who got a referral to this professional institution was no longer able to walk unaided". (Józef Bau, *Time of Desecration*). We continue along ul. Heltmana, where German officials lived during the Płaszów Camp's existence. At ul. Heltmana 22 stands the former **CAMP COMMANDER AMON GOETH'S VILLA** 30. It used to be called the 'red house', and once housed a surgery room for children with tuberculosis. One of the symptoms of Amon Goeth's perversity was his custom of shooting at camp inmates heading for work from behind the curtains of this house. Numerous gatherings of German officials, usually involving heavy drinking, were held here; they were often accompanied by the Rosner brothers, a pair of famous violinists.

We return to the intersection with ul. Abrahama. We turn left before the 'Grey House' and into an unasphalted road (ul. Abrahama), which once ran through the middle of the camp. Nearby we come across a **MONUMENT COMMEMORATING THE FIRST GERMAN EXECUTION IN KRAKÓW OF 13 POLES** 31 on 10th September, 1939.

We go along ul. Abrahama. On the left we can see a hill; it was there that the main camp quarry was situated. Let us try to ascend the path on the left, until we reach a gravelled road; we can have a much better view from up there. We turn left, and several metres on we shall see the site of the former **ROLL-CALL SQUARE** 32, where the camp inmates had to stand for many hours every day. The square also witnessed selections; e.g. the 7th May, 1944 selection when "a health roll-call was held. Each man stripped naked and had to walk in front of Dr Blancke at a distance of 10 m, who decided with a movement of his finger which of the two nearby tables the prisoner was supposed to approach. ...Since the 'call' took a while, the chill forced the Germans to put on additional coats, whereas the naked prisoners were left waiting for their turn" (Bieberstein). About 1,400 men were selected then, and a week later, together with the children of the camp's *Kinderheim*, were sent to Auschwitz to die in gas chambers. Further on the right there were male barracks, and behind them female ones. Polish barracks were situated in a separate part. "The relationships between Polish and Jewish inmates were characterised by friendliness; they helped each other out" – states Bieberstein. On the left, workshop barracks and other camp buildings (a bakery, bath house, etc.) were situated. On the left of the road we can notice a cross erected on the site of a mass grave called the 'Lipowy Hole', the former Austrian fort. We reach an asphalted road and turn left, heading for the monuments visible form here. On the right stands a **MONUMENT COMMEMORATING THE UNKNOWN JEWS** 33. The monument was erected by the Kraków Jews and the commemorative plaque reads: "Here on this site, several thousand Jews were brought from Poland and Hungary, and were tortured, murdered and burnt, between 1943 and 1945. We do not know their names. We shall name them with one word: JEWS. The human tongue lacks words to describe the depth of this atrocity. Its incredible bestiality, ruthlessness and cruelty. We shall name it with one word – HITLERISM. To commemorate the murdered, whose last cry of despair is the silence of this Płaszów cemetery – we pay homage, we, the survivors of the fascist pogrom – the Jews". Nearby there stands another small **MONUMENT COMMEMORATING THE HUNGARIAN JEWESSES** 34, who were kept in the Płaszów Camp in 1944, awaiting to be transferred to the Auschwitz gas chambers. The largest of the monuments was placed in 1964 exactly on the site of the aforementioned 'Hujowa Hill', the former Austrian fortification where mass executions were conducted. The **MONUMENT COMMEMORATING THE MARTYRS** 35 murdered by Nazi slaughterers between 1943 and 1945. We stand on the hill and look towards the camp in the direction of the crossing of the asphalted roads – it was there that hospital barracks were situated, in which the aforementioned Aleksander Bieberstein worked. "Due to the surgical barracks' close proximity to the mass execution site (about 250 m in a straight line), I was often witness to those executions and the accompanying scenes, I heard the threats and swearing of the convicts, I saw the unfortunately failed attempts at self-defence. In one of the transports, a whole wedding party with priest and wedding guests was brought here".

Standing here, at the site of the former Płaszów Camp with thousands of ashes of the murdered, whose last cry of despair is the silence of this Płaszów cemetery, let us muse over the fate of the people whose life came to an end here, and think that they could have been members of our families or ourselves; and let us remember this site and its history.

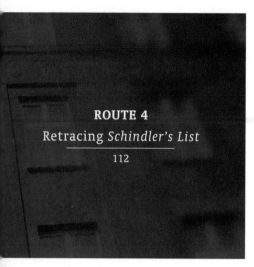

ROUTE 4
Retracing *Schindler's List*

This route takes about 3 hours and visits the places associated with Oskar Schindler's stay in Kraków during the Second World War, as well as with the *Schindler's List* film shot here by Steven Spielberg in 1993. If you can, try to see the film once again before going on this walk, or soon afterwards in order to recognise the sites used in some scenes.

■ ul. Szeroka > ul. Ciemna > ul. Jakuba > ul. Józefa > ul. Bożego Ciała > ul. Bonifraterska > ul. Trynitarska > ul. Krakowska > most Piłsudskiego > ul. Legionów > ul. Kalwaryjska > Rynek Podgórski > ul. Parkowa > Wzgórze Lasoty > ul. Rękawka > ul. Węgierska > ul. Józefińska > ul. Targowa > ul. Lwowska > ul. Traugutta > ul. Lipowa > ul. Kącik > ul. Limanowskiego > ul. Wielicka

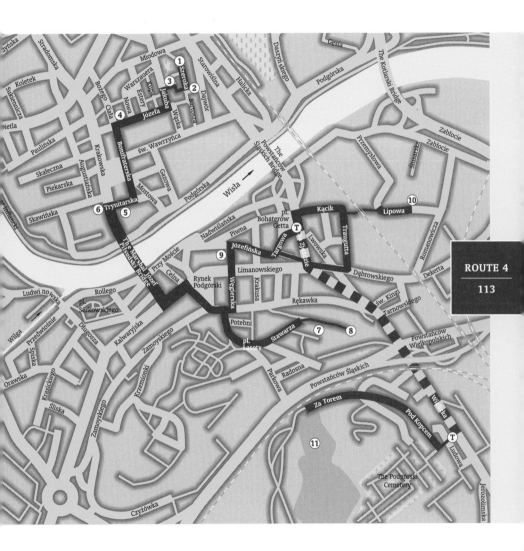

Filming *Schindler's List* here in Kraków was undoubtedly a great event. Soon afterwards, lots of people began arriving to see the location of the film, which was a great eye-opener for people all over the world.

The figure of Oskar Schindler has evoked many controversies (see box p. 32) – both Thomas Keneally in the book and Spielberg in his film present him in a rather idealised manner, and they are often reproached for glorifying 'a good German' in contrast to all those 'bad ones'. On the other hand, Schindler performed a great deed in saving so many lives. When asked why he had done so, he never gave a straightforward answer, and neither did his wife nor the Jews he had saved. Among various hypotheses, there are opinions that he had wished to outwit or ridicule the system; or that under an air of promiscuity he was exhibiting the ability to resist the inhumane atrocitites of those times.

We begin in **UL. SZEROKA** 1. It was here in the film that Plac Zgody from the Kraków Ghetto was recreated. The director's choice was mainly based on the fact that the original former Plac Zgody (now Plac Bohaterów Getta) has undergone significant changes since World War II – numerous modern buildings have been erected. On the other hand, ul. Szeroka has remained unaltered for more than a hundred years, since Kraków was not bombed during the Second World War, and so its urban structure has not been destroyed. Some scenes of everyday ghetto life were shot here, such as conversations while baking potatoes, or registration for forced labour or permission to remain in the ghetto – we might recall the tables with German officers and Jews queueing in front of them. Moreover, scenes of the deportation and liquidation operations were shot here, when Jews had to gather here and then march to the railway station in Prokocim. We ought to bear in mind that all these scenes of deportations and liquidation in reality took place in the German ghetto in Podgórze on the other bank of the Vistula River, at the present Plac Bohaterów Getta, which acted as *Umschlagplatz*. The scene when the commander of the Płaszów Camp, Amon Goeth, appears for the first time, being driven in a car and shown around the ghetto, was also filmed here, as well as the scene when the pharmacy owner, Tadeusz Pankiewicz, tries to rescue a wounded Jewess.

In a small street joining ul. Szeroka with ul. Dajwór, next to the Old Synagogue, the **MAIN GATE** 2 to the ghetto was reconstructed. Next to it other scenes were shot: Jews marching to work, and the moment

Schindlerjuden about Schindler

Jonathan Dresner: "He was an adventurer. He was like an actor who always wanted to be centre stage. He got into a play, and couldn't get out of it".

Mosche Bejski: "Schindler was a drunkard. Schindler was a womanizer. His relations with his wife were bad. He often had not only one but several girlfriends. Everything he did put him in jeopardy. If Schindler had been a normal man, he would not have done what he did".

Danka Dresner: "We owe our lives to him. But I wouldn't glorify a German because of what he did for us. There is no proportion".

Ludwik Feigenbaum: "I don't know what his motives were, even though I knew him very well. I asked him and I never got a clear answer and the film doesn't make it clear either. What's important is that he saved our lives".

Abraham Zuckerman: "The movie didn't show all the little things he did; he came around and greeted you. I had food, protection, and hope".

Ludmilla Pfefferberg-Page: "To know the man was to love him. For us he was a god".

(www.tulane.edu)

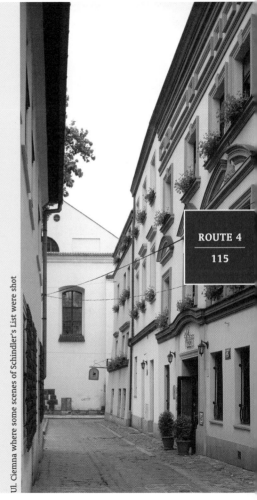

Ul. Ciemna where some scenes of Schindler's List were shot

when Schindler meets two Jewish bankers in a car, who wish to invest in his Enamelware Factory. One of the bankers is the aforementioned 'Last Klezmer of Galicia' – Leopold Kozłowski.

From Szeroka we turn into ul. Ciemna, passing by the only Jewish hotel in Kraków, the Eden Hotel, with a mikvah and kosher food, and reach the corner of **CIEMNA AND JAKUBA STREETS** 3. Let us stop here and look back. We can see suitcases lying on the ground and a few German officers headed by Amon Goeth with dogs running towards us. From ul. Jakuba we can see a young man jumping round the corner, who has just left the sewage. At the sight of the Germans he salutes and says he is a Polish soldier who has received an order to clean the street. They start laughing and it saves his life. This scene was shot right here and the young man in reality was Leopold Pfefferberg-Page, who was saved by Schindler, and who was the originator of the book *Schindler's Ark*. Why? Thomas Kenneally, an Australian writer, says in the preface to his book that in 1980 he visited a luggage store in Beverly Hills, California where he met the store's owner, Leopold Pfefferberg. When the latter heard that Thomas was a writer, he immediately said, "I've got a story for you to write about,"

and Kenneally replied, "No doubt about that, you know that every day several people have stories for me to write about!" But then he heard the account of Oskar Schindler and his salvage of over 1,000 people, and in the 1980s the book was published, on the basis of which *Schindler's List* was made.

The hotel building, although it was a complete ruin in 1993, also played a part in the movie, when the wealthy Nusenbaum family had to desert their luxurious flat for Schindler's sake and move into a flat with four other families. We go along ul. Jakuba, reach ul. Józefa, turn right and after several metres we enter the gate at no. 12. We enter the courtyard at **UL. JÓZEFA 12** 4 (see *Route 3*). It was here that another scene was shot – a mother hides a daughter (Danka Dresner) in a shelter beneath the floor (there was no room for her), and walks down the stairs on the left. But the daughter does not want to be separated from her mother and soon joins her. There are suitcases lying on the ground again and a small boy in a police cap rearranges them. Some German officers come from the opposite side. The boy quickly hides the mother and the daughter beneath the stairs and comes towards the Germans and reports that he has searched the house and there was no one there, thus saving the lives of both women. Liquidation scenes were also shot here, when the German officers searched the flats and threw suitcases and other objects through the windows.

We leave the courtyard and turn left into ul. Bożego Ciała, until we reach Plac Wolnica. Now we will retrace the route the film Jews followed from Kazimierz to the ghetto in Podgórze, walking along the following streets: Bonifraterska, Trynitarska, Krakowska, and the Marshal Józef Piłsudski Bridge. At **UL. TRYNITARSKA** **5** the scene with Polish children shouting, "Goodbye Jews!" was filmed. In the corner building at Skawińska and Krakowska streets stands the **JEWISH COMMUNITY OFFICE** **6**, where the scene with people queueing to the *Judenrat* to get registered for labour, as well as the scene when Schindler finds Icchak Stern and discussed his plans with him, were shot.

Due to Podgórze's modernisation (e.g. the TV tower), it was not possible to film a panoramic view of the former ghetto, therefore during the scenes at the bridge actors and extras walked towards Kazimierz, instead of towards Podgórze. One might say that it was the symbolic return of the Jews to Kazimierz – although obviously cinematic ones.

We leave the bridge and turn left and walk along ul. Legionów and ul. Kalwaryjska, towards Rynek Podgórski. We walk along the eastern side of the square, we ascend

ul. Parkowa, and then turn left into ul. gen. Antoniego Stawarza, which leads up to the **LASOTY HILL** **7**. On the top of the hill we can see a beautiful example of Austrian fortification architecture, the **ŚW. BENEDYKT FORT** **8**, Martello Tower. Next to it, on the left, stands the small mediaeval Church of St. Benedict, one of the oldest in Kraków. Just next to the church, to the right, there is the path from which the film Schindler and his lady friend, Ingrid, on horseback, watched the liquidation of the ghetto and saw the girl in the red coat. This was the only colour that appeared in the whole film. It was then that his spiritual metamorphosis was to take place and he decided to save as many Jews as possible. One might say it was Thomas Keneally's poetic licence used by Spielberg and it is unlikely that something like this could have happened, although there are two ladies (Stella Müller-Madej, *The Girl from Schindler's List*, and Roma Ligocka, *The Girl in the Red Coat*), who claim that they are that girl in the red coat. It needs to be mentioned that during the ghetto's existence the hill was not as bushy as it is today, so the view from here went much further.

We walk down the hill following the same route, turn right into ul. Rękawka and then immediately left into ul. Węgierska.

We cross ul. Limanowskiego and reach ul. Józefińska, where on the left at no. 2 was the aforementioned **LEOPOLD PFEFFERBERG'S HOUSE** 9 . We turn around and walk along ul. Józefińska until we reach ul. Lwowska (we need to cross the tram rails in ul. Na Zjeździe), where we can see one of the two ghetto wall remnants, which also appears in the film. From ul. Lwowska we turn into ul. Dąbrowskiego, and immediately turn left into ul. Traugutta, which was the border street of the ghetto until October 1942. At the end of the street we turn right and walk under the rail viaduct. Then we head straight on for ul. Lipowa 4 where **SCHINDLER'S FACTORY** 10 is located. It is the original enamelware factory building which Oskar Schindler bought in 1939, and the same building appeared in Spielberg's film. On the building's façade there is a plaque commemorating Oskar Schindler, which contains a verse from the Talmud: "He who saves one life, saves the world entire". Medals awarded by Yad Vashem bear the same sentence. Some scenes were shot outside, e.g. when Schindler could not make up his mind which secretary to hire and hires them all (which was not necessarily true), and then has a photograph of himself and all the ladies taken in front of the factory. Scenes inside the factory were filmed in an abandoned enamelware works in Olkusz near Kraków. We can try to have a look through the gate on the left at the preserved staircase, which also 'starred' in the film. Let us recall a young woman who was hiding outside the ghetto with so-called 'Aryan' papers, who came to ask Schindler to take her parents, Jakub and Chana Pearlman, into his factory. When she comes for the first time, she stands at the bottom of this very staircase, next to the porter's office, and Schindler looks down on her from the top of the stairs and refuses to see her. When she comes the second time, she is dressed nicely in some borrowed smart clothes and he does see her, but when she expresses her request he throws her out, saying he is not a charity institution. However, later on we see her again walking along the street in front of the factory, and she notices her parents walking into the factory, which means that he has fulfilled her request.

We return along ul. Lipowa, go under the viaduct and go straight on along ul. Kącik, which leads us to Plac Bohaterów Getta (see p. 98). It was here that all the dramatic events filmed in ul. Szeroka, deportations and the ghetto liquidation, actually took place. The corner building of the square hosts the original Pharmacy 'Under the Eagle', at present the National Remembrance

St Benedict's Church on the Lassoty Hill (from where Schindler watched the liquidation of the ghetto)

Museum. In the square we can get on a no. 3, 9, 13 or 24 tram and get off at the third stop, at Podgórski Cemetery. We cross the street and turn left into ul. Ludowa, which leads to aleja Pod Kopcem. We walk along the avenue named after the nearby prehistoric Krakus Mound, and reach ul. Za Torem, which leads to **LIBAN'S QUARRY** 11, no longer functioning. In 1942, a penal camp, Building Services, was established here, which was closed down in 1944. There were only three barracks here then, but for the film the entire Płaszów camp was reconstructed here. Allan Starski, a prominent art director, built 34 barracks and 11 watchtowers, nearly the most expensive scenery in the history of Polish cinematography. Most camp scenes were filmed here: choosing the girl for the house servant at Amon Goeth's villa, where the commander chooses the only one who does not volunteer, Helen Hirsch; the scene when Goeth orders the shooting of Diana Reiter, an engineer who has given instructions to relay the barrack foundations, and then orders to follow her instructions. The petrifying Amon Goeth was rather faithfully depicted in the movie, although when you hear or read memoirs of the survivors, his bestiality is beyond description. He used cruel methods to force people to work faster and more efficiently.

Once he ordered a certain building assignment to be conducted at unrealistically short notice, and then he imprisoned the wife and daughter of the engineer Zygmunt Grünberg, threatening that if the job were not completed by the set deadline, they would both die. It is hard to imagine what the man felt then. Thanks to the extraordinary effort of all his fellow inmates, who worked incessantly for a few days, the task was completed on time, and both women survived.

Some roll-calls and the 1944 selection scenes were also shot here. Unfortunately, nothing has been preserved of that scenery, and the site itself is not easily accessible. There is a monument commemorating the prisoners tortured and murdered here during World War II.

For those who are not exhausted yet, there is another option: if you follow ul. Za Torem, after a few hundred metres, you reach the territory of the former Płaszów Camp.

The *Schindler's List* route comes to an end here. It needs to be said that the film quite faithfully depicts the events of those days, nevertheless it is not entirely objective and does not show all sides of the coin. All in all, it is a film which has been a great eye-opener to people all over the world and which will definitely prevent us from forgetting the tragic events of the Holocaust.

The panoramic view of Kraków Ghetto in Podgórze

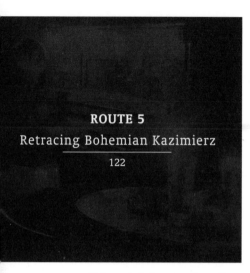

This route takes you along the most important spots of social-artistic Kazimierz.

The tour may start with some afternoon coffee and last to the very dawn.

For a social meeting: Singer (ul. Estery) > Warsztat (ul. Isaaca) > ul. Ciemna > ul. Szeroka > Ptaszyl and Transylwania in ul. Szeroka > ul. Podbrzezie > La Habana and Propaganda in ul. Miodowa > Lokator in ul. Krakowska > ul. Meiselsa > Mleczarnia in ul. Meiselsa > ul. Józefa > Eszeweria in ul. Józefa > Kolanko No. 6 in ul. Józefa > Kawiarnia Naukowa in ul. Jakuba > Plac Nowy > Alchemia > Les Couleurs > Królicze Oczy

For a concert or a cultural event: Klezmer-Hois > Drukarnia na Kazimierzu > Alchemia > Scena EL-JOT

For breakfast and morning coffee: Plac Nowy and Les Couleurs > Proces Parzenia Kafki > Kawa pod Kogutkiem > Café Młynek in Plac Wolnica

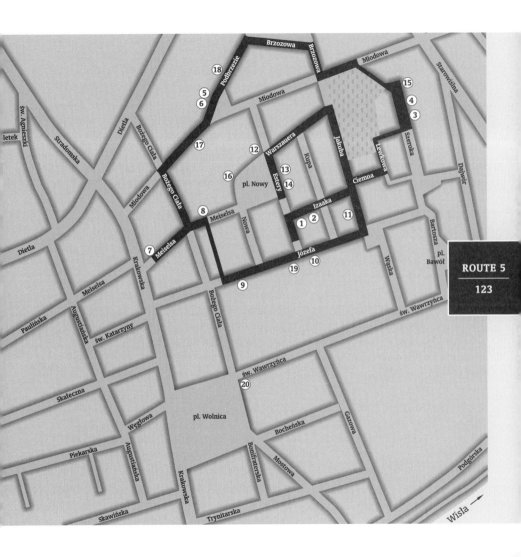

It is Kraków's Kazimierz that nowadays possesses the bohemian atmosphere that Kraków once boasted. A new social-artistic centre has been developing here for a few years now, which is manifested by numerous effervescent cafés bustling with 'spiritual' life. It is too early to evaluate if Kazimierz has already become or will become the new venue of contemporary bohemian Kraków. No distinctly separate group of artists and writers leading free and eccentric lifestyles, creating modern artistic circles such as the *Zielony Balonik*, an early twentieth-century Polish cabaret, Theatre Cricot and Cricot 2 or *Piwnica pod Baranami*, has emerged yet. There are still too few artistic and cultural events, exhibitions, and underground events taking place in Kazimierz. Nonetheless, the mysterious atmosphere of this quarter has been inspiring and attracting writers, poets, actors, journalists, photographers and musicians who meet in their favourite places. They say there is a bit of Prague, Paris or Berlin in Kazimierz and compare its atmosphere to Žižkovo, Saint-Germain-des-Prés and Kreuzberg, or to some picturesque locales of world literature.

In Kazimierz, I feel like a character out of Bruno Schulz's stories. Kazimierz lives its own, magical rhythm.

Mateusz Zaręba, musician, vocalist in the band ZOOID, a Kazimierz resident

Therefore, we highly recommend retracing bohemian Kazimierz and visiting its artistic cafés, pubs and clubs – cultural events venues and beer 'pump-rooms'. The following descriptions are a subjective selection of places with the highest concentration of so-called 'Kazimierz atmosphere'. It needs to be emphasised here that this route was designed on the basis of opinions of a number of Kazimierz residents and Kraków 'old-timers' – musicians, actors, journalists, media people and all others possessing artistic souls who have fallen in love with this place. It is they who will lead the reader through the magical nooks of Kazimierz to discover its atmosphere. However, you should not rely entirely on their opinions – you are more than welcome to establish your own café route and find your own favourite places. We begin this walk in the late afternoon or evening. At first, we shall visit the best places for social meetings, where, surrounded by stirring music and Kazimierz's magical atmosphere, we can feel time stop.

Later on we shall visit a few musical and theatrical venues, where regular concerts of klezmer, blues, jazz, and rock music, as well as theatre performances and film showings, are held. Our walk will end in the early hours in a few cafés, where you can drink your morning coffee, have breakfast, read newspapers and recall moments spent in Kazimierz.

We begin our walk at Singer – the very first artistic pub in Kazimierz.

The famous and already legendary **SINGER** 1 at ul. Estery 22 is the oldest artistic pub in Kazimierz, where you come for a meeting as if to an old friend's house. Its three rooms are very economically furnished – 'Singer' sewing-machines are used as tables for the guests, and there are a few larger tables and old mirrors. The interior is rather sombre, but romantic, lit by candlelight and a lamp with a red lamp-shade next to the bar. The place is overwhelmed by an atmosphere from the pre-vious century, thick with conversations and cigarette smoke (although the smoke concen-tration has been significantly reduced since an air-conditioning system was installed here, which definitely took away some of the place's charm, but is healthier for the staff). It is a favourite venue of Kraków artistic circles. Singer is open late into the night and always crowded, mainly by regulars, some-times accompanied by their dogs. You can often hear the moody music of Jacques Brel, Frank Sinatra, as well as Flamenco music or Almodovar's film soundtracks. Connoisseurs praise Singer's atmosphere at all times of the day (it opens at 9 am): early, dreamy af-ternoons, bustling evenings, or late at night with the most persistent customers. At Singer you can even dance, and the windows of the

Singer's unique atmosphere

The lovely 'instrument shelterhouse' at Warsztat

first room overlook the magical Plac Nowy. Draught Żywiec, cherry brandy and slivovitz are most popular here.

Kazimierz. Diversity. Distinction. It is not just a set of old houses and a few squares; it is a perfect combination of the past and present. It is a relationship of people and places, those of the past and of today.

Katarzyna Pilitowska, head of promotion at the Kraków branch of the *Gazeta Wyborcza* newspaper, resident of Kazimierz

We are at the corner of Estery and Izaaka Streets. We turn into ul. Izaaka. We stop at no. 3, at the **WARSZTAT** 2 café, called the 'instrument shelter house'. The interior is decorated with musical instruments, and it seems as if they play music to soothe your soul. This venue is a union of poetry and music. It is a romantic café consisting of two rooms – crimson and navy blue. There are several dark tables with candles on them, instruments hanging below the ceiling, and mirrors on the walls. The bar, made from a grand piano, attracts our attention. The piano next to the bar is not a prop; twice a week, in the evening, a great pianist, Mariusz Hrabia, plays mostly jazz standards here. It is cosy to sip a beer or a glass of wine here any time of the year, but especially in winter when the streets of Kazimierz are covered with snow. A beautiful view of the Isaac Synagogue is visible from here. From time to time concerts, exhibition launches and poetic meetings are held here. Draught Żywiec is served in jugs, and coffee tastes better with nut cake. Even the plates have musical notes on them.

Unlike in Prague, you can find peace in Kazimierz, and can 'stop' for a moment. One may wonder who from the energetic artistic circles wandering around Kazimierz may be the future Bruno Schulz... There is a bit of Prague, Jerusalem and Paris in it.

Daniel Mourek, resident and town councillor of Prague, vegetarian, Prague underground lover, Central European Greenways Coordinator

We walk along ul. Izaaka, cross ul. Jakuba and find ourselves in the romantic ul. Ciemna with a few spots characterised by – typical for contemporary Kazimierz – strong contrasts. Dilapidated buildings neighbour on recently renovated hotels and restaurants. The saddest view is at the corner of Ciemna and Lewkowa Streets. Nevertheless, all these picturesque and photogenic nooks call places from Dostoyevsky's prose to mind.

There are, Nastenka, though you may not know it, strange nooks in Petersburg. It seems as though the same sun as shines for all Petersburg people does not peep into those spots, but some

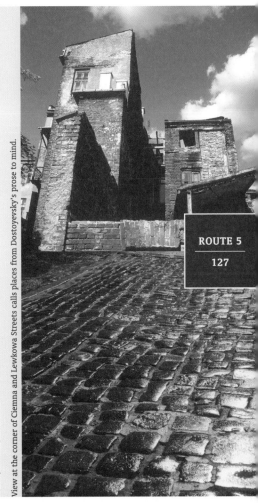

View at the corner of Ciemna and Lewkowa Streets calls places from Dostoyevsky's prose to mind.

The open-air café in front of Ptaszyl

other different new one, bespoken expressly for those nooks, and it throws a different light on everything. ... Well, life is a mixture of something purely fantastic, fervently ideal, with something (alas, Nastenka!) dingily prosaic and ordinary, not to say incredibly vulgar.

Fyodor Dostoyevsky, *White Nights, A Sentimental Story of The Diary of A Dreamer*

We turn into ul. Lewkowa, which leads to ul. Szeroka – where all the revitalisation of Kazimierz began in the early 1990s. It is worth knowing that at no. 26 Jerzy Panek, graphic designer, painter, and author of magical woodcuts and etchings, once lived. On the other side of the street you can see a row of cafés with tables outside in the summer filled with Kraków locals and tourists. We will visit Ptaszyl and Transylwania.

PTASZYL 3, at ul. Szeroka 10, is a nest of weird 'birdos' living on tree branches below the ceiling or sprouting up straight from the floor. Birdos are strange, undefined creatures which take on the shape of masks, lanterns, bells and even suitcases. A portrait of a large, mad birdo hangs on the front wall. Orange walls and blue ceilings, candles on the tables and colour bulbs create a warm and optimistic mood for the interior. A wardrobe with the plaque *Proprieté privée. Defense d'entrer* is built into the wall. Is there a mysterious world of birdos behind that wardrobe? It calls C. S.

Lewis's magical world of Narnia to mind. In the wintertime a fireplace heats the interior.

This venue is quite busy in the evening and rather drowsy during the day. Photography exhibitions; modern music, e.g. modern electro-jazz, ambient. Draught Pilsner, Tyskie and Lech.

TRANSYLWANIA 4 , at no. 9, is a small café inspired by mysterious Transylvania and its stereotypical vampires headed by Dracula. But don't be afraid – the place is well-equipped with wooden stakes and garlic hanging above the bar, entrance door and tables. Instructions on how to deal with a vampire's body are available at the bar. Gloomy interior, coffee-beige walls, a few tables covered with curtains. You can also sit in a wardrobe, but beware of being absorbed into the world of darkness. The wall behind the bar is highlighted in red, with numerous portraits of Dracula. There is a selection of draught beer – Żywiec, Heineken, Beamish, Cider Blackthorn and Scottish Ale Belhaven; as well as an extensive selection of teas brewed in teapots, and flavourful and fiery coffees (with alcohol). Snacks: toasted sandwiches, buttered popcorn and nachos with cheese.

From ul. Szeroka we enter ul. Miodowa and turn into ul. Brzozowa, and then into ul. Podbrzezie, which joins ul. Miodowa, creating

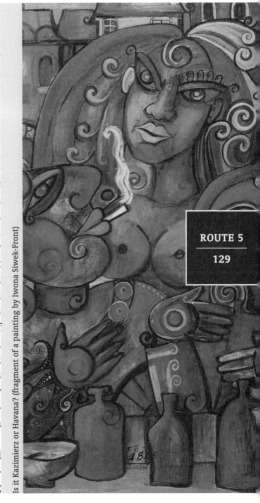

Is it Kazimierz or Havana? (fragment of a painting by Iwona Siwek-Front)

a lovely passage with a few cafés. The two oldest and most famous ones are Cuban La Habana and Propaganda.

LA HABANA `5`, at ul. Miodowa 22, is a pub à la Cuba, open from 9 am *hasta el ultimo cliente*. There are two rooms: one with a mezzanine, the other with the bar. Warm lighting, soft pastel orange walls and a few palms in pots create the atmosphere of Buena Vista Social Club songs depicting life in small Cuban town streets: Alto Cedro, Marcané, Cueto or Mayarí. We can see some photographs of Cuba, and a Cuba Feliz film poster on the walls. Photography exhibitions in a small gallery on the mezzanine, slide showings and spontaneous parties take place here. Draught Żywiec, colourful beer cocktails, Hemingway cocktails, Cuban cigars and snacks, such as *pollo con salsa ticante*.

De Alto Cedro voy para Marcané
Luego a Cueto voy para Mayarí
The song 'Chan Chan' from Buena Vista Social Club

PROPAGANDA `6`, at ul. Miodowa 20, is referred to as a museum of social realism, since it hosts a selection of tokens from the previous epoch, such as informative or warning-instructional signs (e.g. "All women working at the machine must wear protective headscarves"), propaganda signboards, posters and advertisements (e.g. valid meat coupon pattern), pennons and flags. The interior, lit by red bulbs, is decorated with old radios, uniforms, portraits of Lenin, a Trabant bonnet built into the wall, a hammer and sickle, and so on. The pub has expanded into the cellar, which resembles a coal mine with a miner mannequin at the entrance. The pub owners say the pub came into being on the one hand due to some nostalgia for the times of youth in a gloomy communist country, in which we somehow managed to live and have fun, on the other hand in order to ridicule that system – its ideological hypocrisy, sheer stupidity, and absurdity. Propaganda celebrates communist holidays that no longer exist, and hosts concerts of Russian virtuosos. The regulars' favourite resting corner is the one with red artificial leather 'stylish' armchairs. Darts, draught Żywiec, cocktails and communist-style snacks, such as '*Siwucha* with Pickle', 'Rabid Dog', and bread with lard.

We walk along ul. Miodowa, turn left into ul. Bożego Ciała and reach ul. Meiselsa. On the corner between ul. Meiselsa and ul. Krakowska is Lokator [Tenant], and at the other end of the street, near Plac Nowy, we will pop into Mleczarnia [Dairy], but by no means for a glass of milk.

LOKATOR `7` (ul. Krakowska 10, entrance in ul. Meiselsa) or *Le Locataire*, as in the Roman Polański film, advertises itself as "a café, pub and gallery" in one with a "chimerical and artistic atmosphere". We are welcomed by a large signboard with a fairy aeroplane from the "Artist in Space" series, and we feel as if we are entering the world of Antoine de Saint-Exupéry's books. It is a tiny, cosy place with a bar at the entrance; the bartenders often read books or play scrabble. You immediately feel at home here. Crimson walls, dark furniture, candles on the tables, jazz (traditional or modern). The interior seems 'classic', but there is something unique in it that draws you in and makes you come back. Lokator hosts regular photography, graphic design, and drawing exhibitions, book launches, concerts, as well as the 'Free Form Radio Show' cycle promoting independent world music. Draught Warka and Żywiec; cocktails: 'Lokator', 'Sąsiedzi'; student discounts on beer. Lokator's specialty is chimerical hot chocolate with whipped cream and a pinch of chili.

MLECZARNIA 8 , at ul. Meiselsa 20, also known as 'No Name' since there is no signboard at the entrance, is an exceptionally social and musical venue that 'takes you in'. Mleczarnia's interior is filled with music, which does not disturb conversations but is a significant part of being here. Stylish interior, purple walls, lace tablecloths, candlelight, plenty of antiques and old photos, a winter fireplace. Both the interior design and the pub's atmosphere are a perfect harmony of the past and present. The pub is open late into the night and usually crowded with people until the end; the bartenders also participate in the social life here. A wide selection of music – rock, jazz, klezmer, French and Spanish music depending on the mood of the day, weather, guests or atmosphere. From time to time, when guests are full of energy, the bartenders play dance music and the cosy corners of Mleczarnia are filled not only with singing but also dancing. Opposite the pub, in the courtyard between ul. Meiselsa and Józefa, tables are put out in the summertime. Draught Żywiec, a wide selection of coffee and delicious hot chocolate. Sweet specialties: apples in caramel and nut cake. We turn into the courtyard between Meiselsa and Józefa Streets considered the most picturesque courtyard of Kazimierz. The Youth Cultural Club used to be here, and it was Kazimierz children's favourite playground. Today the courtyard is filled with open-air cafés. It looks enchanting, but for those with memories of the old days it has lost its magical charm.

We enter ul. Józefa, considered exceptional and magical by many.

Ul. Józefa is 'Kazimierz in a pill', an exploding composition of diverse worlds coexisting and creating an eclectic harmony. Small trade, ar-

The only pierogi bar in Kazimierz – U Vincenta

tistic life and tourist traffic all thrive here. Apart from small shops with 'everything', 'traditional' hairdressers, antique, souvenir and jewellery shops, ul. Józefa hosts a number of galleries promoting contemporary art, art naïf or Jewish art, the most renowned being the Szalom Gallery (no. 16), and d'Art Naïf (no. 11). There are also a number of cafés, restaurants, e.g. delicious dumplings at U Vincenta (no. 11), and luxurious hotels; as well as the only bicycle rental service in Kazimierz, Dwa Koła (no. 5), with stylish bicycles straight from Holland (all the above are described in detail in Practical Information).

In the evening you need to stop at Eszeweria for mulled wine in winter or a cold drink in summer, and at Kolanko No. 6 for a pint of beer and delicious pancakes.

ESZEWERIA 9, at ul. Józefa 9, is a unique, remarkable and poetic café. Located off the beaten pub track, it allows you to escape the town's turmoil, hide in your favourite corner with a book, play dice with friends or discuss poetry, theatre, and Kraków with the bartenders. Three cosy rooms, rustic walls, a few pieces of antique furniture, an original bar à la cupboard. Walls covered with regular photography exhibitions, tables with candles and fresh flowers, drinks served in beautiful dishes: sophisticated glasses, flower-painted mugs, and porcelain cups. Care for detail is visible at every step here. The café is named after a plant native to Central America (Lat. *Echeveria* – after the 19th-century Mexican botanical illustrator). This exotic plant with thick, fleshy leaves and iridescent leaf rosettes is often called the 'stone rose'. The mystery and beauty of a foreign plant perfectly reflect the atmosphere of the café, especially appreciated by women. As rumour has it, the place was designed by women, and you can sense the female spirit here. Whoever pops in once, will definitely come back.

In the summertime you are welcome to the backyard for a cold drink. The selection of music depends on the guests and the mood – sung poetry, Nick Cave, the *Amélie* soundtrack.

Perhaps it is not appropriate to write about the intimate nooks of the café, but it would be a pity not to mention the bathroom, which is very romantically and originally designed. It is said to be a Kraków tourist attraction already…

Draught Żywiec, bottled Pilsner Urquell. Mulled wine with herbs and fruit, original soft cocktails ('Cat's Paw', 'Sunrise') or cold drinks. The Chilean wine 'Echeverria' (Merlot, Cabernet Sauvignon and Chardonnay). A wide selection of tea brewed in teapots.

At ul. Józefa 17, a cosy pub called **KOLANKO NO. 6** 🔟 is located. You pop in here for a cup of coffee, a beer or, when hungry, for the famous house pancakes with diverse fillings, from spinach, broccoli and chicken to nuts and honey, or for tasty soups, such as onion soup with cheese and toast. The interior resembles the atmosphere of a Paris café: photos of café and restaurant windows, stylish lanterns, walls resembling an old mansion's façade in a dark olive shade. It feels moody and modern. The bar is made of bricks, the tables and chairs of fair wood, there are metal lamps above the tables, a shelf with books and magazines to read, photographs and travel magazines. Classic jazz, blues, reggae and old rock. Draught Tyskie. Kolanko's speciality is cappuccino with cream and hot chocolate with whipped cream.

We turn into ul. Jakuba, and just round the corner we pop into **KAWIARNIA NAUKOWA** 11 at no. 29. Austere interior, walls covered with stones, stained glass windows. Intellectual-casual atmosphere in the rhythm of reggae. A social mixture of underground-oriented people interested in ecology and anthropology. Concerts, philosophical-literary lectures and discussions take place here, as well as social meetings accompanied by drum music, reggae, rock and modern music. The pub's speciality is natural coffee straight from Mexico, 100% ecological, grown in the shade on a small farm, far away from large plantations, dried in the Mesoamerican sun and bought according to fair trading rules (directly from the manufacturer). It has an excellent aroma; unfortunately, it is brewed and not served in a real espresso coffee machine. Draught Okocim and Carlsberg.

We turn into ul. Warszauera and reach Plac Nowy. This characteristic spot of the present Kazimierz that never sleeps is a renowned social-café centre. Plac Nowy, also known as 'Jewish Square', is the heart of Kazimierz. From dawn till dusk a colourful, changeable life full of contrasts takes place, while more and more 'trendy' or 'cult' venues come into being. In the evening it is bustling and noisy, especially in summer when people sit in the open-air cafés or at the stalls in the middle of the square, which, unfortunately, often leads to conflicts between pub owners and residents.

Apart from sitting in the nearby pubs for hours it has also become trendy to have a quick snack at one of the joints (Endzior, Namaxa, Bar Oko and U Danusi) in the round building in the middle of the square. *Zapiekanka ze szczypiorkiem* [toasted baguette with cheese, mushrooms and chives] is especially popular at Namaxa.

Kazimierz is the only coherent quarter in Central Europe with a specific local character. Unlike Prague, which is mainly a tourist attraction with little connection with everyday life, in Kazimierz you come across a local marketplace, cosy cafés and bars, grocery shops neighboured by luxurious restaurants and hotels. Pop in for a delicious coffee, order a vegetarian chive toast and let life pass near you...
Daniel Mourek

The interwar atmosphere of existentialism can be found in Alchemia and Les Couleurs.

In the evening we visit Plac Nowy to pop into a few pubs to meet friends, or to attend a concert or cultural event. We will come back in the morning to observe the other side of this typical Kazimierz spot.

ALCHEMIA 12, at ul. Estery 5, is an existential venue with a rich spiritual and artistic soul. The mysterious study of alchemy is extremely popular. Perhaps some even hope to find the philosopher's stone or a potion for immortality? The four and a half rooms and a cellar host a pub, gallery, theatre, cinema and concert stage. It sparkles with life, and more and more distinguished cultural events are held here, from photography and art exhibitions, through concerts, cabarets, theatre performances, original film festivals (such as the recent festivals of Hungarian films and Cuban musicals), to poetic-literary meetings.

Alchemia an existential venue with a rich and artistic soul

An alchemist's studio

The interior is filled with the spirit of old remote times, hidden secrets and mysticism. At the same time, Alchemia lives a contemporary life. For some, the venue is positively inspiring, for others it is decadent and gloomy. The weird and impenetrable atmosphere of Alchemia is a key to its originality and 'unforgettableness'. You definitely need to consider the rich cultural-artistic contribution of the venue.

The famous **LES COULEURS** 13, at ul. Estery 10, is a mini-Paris in Kazimierz, a reminiscence of Saint-Germain-des-Prés. The pub is friendly, optimistic and moody. It has something of the Montmartre café where the film Amélie Poulain worked. Les Couleurs is indeed colourful. Bedside lamps with colourful shades on the tables, the bar lit by red and yellow bulbs. It is nice to sit either at the small cosy tables, or at the long couch near the wall for ten people, or at the equally long bar. The walls are covered with French posters advertising old museum and gallery exhibitions, concerts and theatre performances in Paris, as well as with paintings by Henrie de Toulouse-Lautrec and motifs of the Paris underground. The cork board features a photo account of the May International Soup Festival at Plac Nowy, which was begun at the pub owner's initiative, and photos of the same festival in Lille. French music, traditional and modern jazz. Draught Żywiec, cocktails, such as 'Kiss in Colours' (cherry brandy with grapefruit juice), and freshly pressed orange or grapefruit juice.

At ul. Estery 14 we can pop into **KRÓLICZE OCZY** 14. This cosy café is especially favoured by couples or small groups of friends. The orange interior is decorated with 1930s photographs, sometimes funny erotic photos with *królicze oczy* [red eyes]. Mirrors, tables with bedside lamps and comfortable couches. A small library features daily newspapers and books by Joseph Conrad and George Orwell. Chess, draughts, and other board games are at the guests' disposal. Funky, modern jazz and ambient music are played here. The café is open till the small hours; sometimes it is the last place to close at Plac Nowy, if not in Kazimierz.

From here we can see Singer, where we started and where we will end our social-artistic pub route. Now we shall visit places recommended for those seeking music and theatre in Kazimierz. We will begin with the sounds closest to Kazimierz: Jewish music in Klezmer-Hois. Later on we will pop into Drukarnia na Kazimierzu for a jazz or blues concert.

MUSIC

KLEZMER-HOIS 15 , the 'Klezmer House' is a Galician Jewish restaurant, hotel and klezmer music and theatre centre with a lovely interior. It is located in the former Great Mikvah at ul. Szeroka 6. Every night at 8 pm a live, traditional Jewish music concert is held (we can hear bands such as Kuzmir, the Yaro Klezmer Band, the Reiner Trio, the Max Klezmer Band and Olga). From time to time, musical-poetic performances take place, which, according to art director Leopold Kozłowski, are linked with the best traditions of Jewish theatre.

When the Austeria restaurant in Kazimierz opened, I said to myself, this is a place where music should be revived. Here in Kazimierz. This atmosphere, its apparent calmness, those dilapidated buildings, these cobblestones that

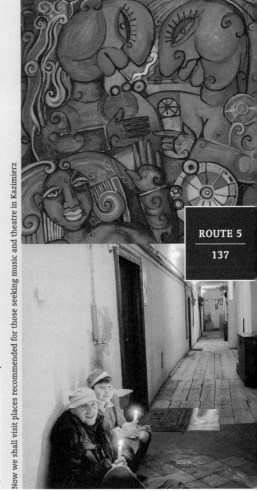

witnessed so much misery – in other words, it was Kazimierz that forced me to do it. It would not leave me alone. And the music was revived. Wojtek Ornat, head of Klezmer-Hois, suggested I record a concert, and I played the first Klezmer concert at his piano. And this is how my genuine creative work started – not only creative, but also educational. It was Hanukkah in 1992.

I am ein Galicjaner, interview with Leopold Kozłowski in: Beata Matkowska-Święs, *Krakowskie gadanie*, Wydawnictwo Literackie, Kraków 2001

DRUKARNIA NA KAZIMIERZU 16, at Plac Nowy 8, is a well-known social-musical venue with regular blues, jazz, and rock concerts, as well as dance parties with pop, rock and blues. Live concerts of Polish and foreign bands are organised here. Drukarnia na Kazimierzu is a two-level pub. Downstairs there is a cellar with a stage and a bar for nearly 100 people. Good acoustics and a club atmosphere provide an excellent base for an evening concert with a pint of beer (draught Okocim and Carlsberg). The ground floor offers space for social meetings with large groups of friends. Bright and spacious interior with walls covered with large reproductions of magazine articles and front pages. You can also encounter items associated with the pub's name [Publishing House] such as parts of old printing presses. A bustling, vital, crowded place, ideal for an intense night in the thunder of jazz or blues.

THEATRE IN KAZIMIERZ

There are still too few theatre events in Kazimierz, but we need to mention a few stages open recently for Melpomene lovers' sake. Let us visit artistic Alchemia once again, and then the Scena EL-JOT theatre.

ALCHEMIA 12 has recently opened an artistic cellar with a stage where many interesting and remarkable cultural events have been taking place: theatre performances, cabarets, theatre song and sung poetry festivals, and theme film festivals.

At ul. Miodowa 15 the cosy, musical **SCENA EL-JOT** 17 is located, established in 1991 by Jadwiga Leśniak-Jankowska, actress, choreographer and professor at the Kraków State Theatre Academy. Theatre performances shown here combine word, gesture, stage movement, dance and music in a sublime and harmonious manner. Stage images take us into the world of mysticism, joy, excitement and poetry. They explore cultural identity, traditions and customs, especially alluding to old Polish, Central European, and Kraków culture as well as the Jewish roots of Kazimierz.

MORNING COFFEE AND BREAKFAST IN A PLEASANT ATMOSPHERE

We welcome the morning in Kazimierz at Plac Nowy. From the early hours, trading and life flourish here. In a pleasant market hum from Monday to Saturday we can get fresh fruit and vegetables, and in the round building in the centre of the marketplace, fresh meat and dairy products. We can feel the specific atmosphere of the place on Tuesday and Friday when a bird market is held, and on Saturday during the antique trade. However, the spot is the most crowded on Sunday, when Plac Nowy turns into a large open-air flea market.

The best post from which to observe Plac Nowy's morning life is **LES COULEURS** 13, already known to us from our night adventure, open from 7 am (the earliest in Kazimierz!). This is an excellent spot for breakfast, morning coffee and reading both Polish and French newspapers. Breakfast features fresh rolls, bread, cheese, cottage cheese, ham and vegetables. You can also order a coffee with a classic croissant or chocolate cake. The café is especially busy on Saturday and Sunday mornings, when the antique and clothes markets take place.

Well-brewed coffee is also served in **PROCES PARZENIA KAFKI** 18, at ul. Podbrzezie 2, a tiny café open at 8:30 am serving breakfast and hot meals (if you fancy an early lunch).

The menu offers mostly pancakes (the café's speciality) with tuna, spinach, cheese, or house 'Kafka' pancakes, as well as *cholent*,

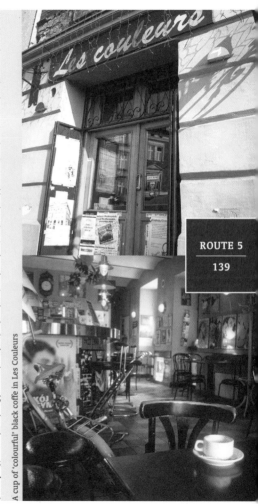

A cup of 'colourful' black coffe in Les Couleurs

'Love messangers' in Kazimierz

lasagne, spaghetti, and şalads. The café features a fireplace, jazz radio and mini library monopolised by several copies of *The Trial* by Franz Kafka, whose portrait hangs above the door.

A 'small, black' coffee is also served at **KAWA POD KOGUTKIEM** [19] at ul. Józefa 11. It is a tiny coffee shop open at 9 am. An extensive selection of coffee from Madagascar, Brazil, and Cameroon, and various blends and flavours to choose from (e.g. coconut or cinnamon). You can also order a coffee 'to go'. The interior is decorated with old espresso coffee machines, coffee grinders and figures, sculptures and pictures of *kogutki* [tiny cocks]. On the wall you can see old photos of the building at no. 11 (it once housed a hairdresser's). It is pleasant to sit on a green couch or armchair watching the drowsy morning life of ul. Józefa. It is a shame that instead of music we are accompanied by... TV.

We end up at sleepy, but picturesque, Plac Wolnica. An exuberant artistic life does not thrive here yet, but Kazimierz lovers are certain that the time will come for Plac Wolnica, possessing huge, unexploited potential. On the corner of the square, at the crossroads of ul. Bożego Ciała and ul. św. Wawrzyńca, the first harbour of local bohemian circles is located – the artistic **CAFÉ MŁYNEK** [20] (Plac Wolnica 7). This cosy café-bar and art gallery, open at 9 am on weekdays and at 10 am at weekends, likes to present itself as "a café in the heart of Kraków's Kazimierz". The interior of this "artistic, grinding melting pot" is decorated with painting, graphic and photography exhibitions which the café is famous for, especially among the Academy of Fine Arts circles. The café has hosted exhibitions of numerous artists, both mature and debutants, both local and national.

We sit at Młynek, drinking coffee and reading today's papers. Before we realise it, the morning has turned into afternoon, and it is nearly time to begin another magical evening in Kazimierz.

Practical Information

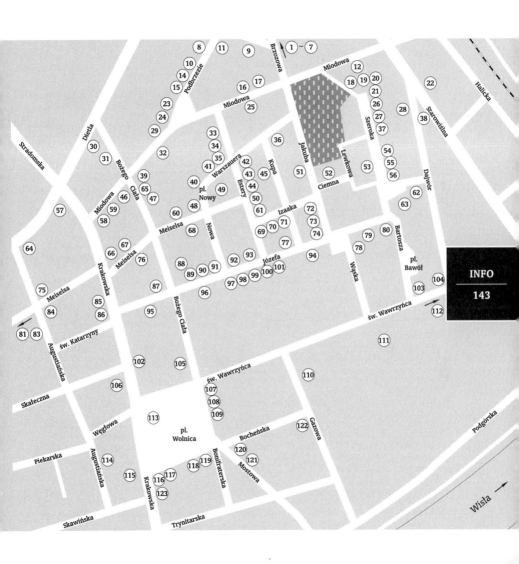

Here is some useful and practical information about Kazimierz. We need to emphasise, however, that the Kazimierz landscape is constantly changing, so it is very likely that soon some new cafés, pubs, restaurants or galleries will come into being that will not be included in the following list, or worse, some of the described ones may cease to exist.

WHERE TO STAY

As far as places to stay are concerned, we face a small problem, since there is not much cheap accommodation here; the number of hotels is impressive for such a small area, but the prices, unfortunately, cannot be described as low.

HOTELS

ASTORIA HOTEL
ul. Józefa 24, tel: (+48-12) 432 50 10, 0 801 800 058, fax: (+48-12) 432 50 20
e-mail: hotelastoria@w.polsce, http://www.astoriahotel.pl
This recently-opened, luxurious hotel offers accommodation for 65 persons in air-conditioned rooms equipped with a bathroom, satellite TV, radio and telephone. It also offers conference rooms, a fitness studio, sauna, bar and a restaurant serving Polish and international cuisine, as well as a guarded parking space underground. The hotel charges 65 EUR for a single room, 82 EUR for a double, and at weekends the prices go down by 10 EUR. Breakfast is included in the price.

EDEN HOTEL
ul. Ciemna 15, tel: (+48-12) 430 65 65, fax: (+48-12) 430 67 67
e-mail: eden@holeleden.pl http://www.holeleden.pl
This lovely hotel situated in the heart of the former Jewish Kazimierz is the only Jewish hotel in Kraków. It houses a *mikvah*, ritual bath house, there is a *mezuzah* box fixed on the doorposts, and kosher food is served here. All 27 rooms (77 persons) are equipped with a bathroom, satellite TV, telephone and Internet access. The hotel charges 80 USD for a single room in high season (April - October), and 105 USD for a double, low season 48 USD and 70 USD respectively. You can have a beer or try some good alcoholic drinks at the Ye Olde Goat Pub located in the labyrinthine 16th-century cellars, where you can also have a go at karaoke on Thursday.

ESTER HOTEL
ul. Szeroka 20, 31-053 Kraków, tel: (+48-12) 429 11 88, fax: (+48-12) 429 12 33
e-mail: biuro@hotel-ester.krakow.pl, http://www.hotel-ester.krakow.pl
Opened in 1998, situated near the Old Synagogue, the hotel offers accommodation for 75 people in 32 air-conditioned rooms equipped with a bathroom, satellite TV and telephone. The air-conditioned restaurant on the ground floor serves European and Jewish cuisine. An unguarded car park is available in front of the hotel and a guarded car park 50 m away. In high season a single room costs 240 zł, a double 280 zł.

KAZIMIERZ HOTEL
ul. Miodowa 16, tel: (+48-12) 421 66 29, fax: (+48-12) 422 28 84
e-mail: hotel@hk.com.pl, http://www.hk.com.pl
Situated in the vicinity of the Reform Synagogue, the hotel offers accommodation for 85 people (35 rooms). Each room is equipped with a bathroom, satellite TV and telephone, some are air-

conditioned. The air-conditioned restaurant (150 persons) offers international cuisine. The hotel features three conference rooms with basic facilities. In high season the prices are as follows (including breakfast): single – 60 EUR, double – 70 EUR. At weekends prices go down by 5 EUR; discounts if booked via the Internet. Children under 12 stay in the hotel free of charge.

REGENT HOTEL
ul. Bożego Ciała 19, tel: (+48-12) 430 62 34, tel./fax: (+48-12) 430 59 77
e-mail: info@rthotels.com.pl, http://www.rthotels.com.pl
Located in a historical mansion in the heart of Kazimierz, the hotel features a unique atmosphere with stylish interiors. All 35 rooms are equipped with a bathroom, satellite TV and telephone, and the restaurant located in the cellars serves a wide selection of tasty meals. The hotel can accommodate 78 persons; it provides childcare, and banquets, organises conferences. In high season rates range from 70 EUR for a single room to 100 EUR for a double. Prices include breakfast and go down by 10% at weekends.

SECESJA HOTEL
ul. Paulińska 24, tel: (+48-12) 430 74 64, 430 74 46, fax: (+48-12) 430 74 05
e-mail: hotel@hotelsecesja.krakow.pl, http://www.hotelsecesja.krakow.pl
Located opposite the historical Pauline monastery on Skałka, this modern hotel offers 20 double rooms (104 EUR), 4 single (82 EUR) and 2 suites (145 EUR); each room is air-conditioned and equipped with a bathroom, satellite TV and telephone. Guests can count on professional service and a friendly atmosphere. Price includes breakfast; groups can negotiate the prices, which go down at weekends and in low season. The hotel also offers three conference rooms, which can accommodate from 12 to 60 people.

GUEST ROOMS

AKIE GUEST ROOMS
ul. Mostowa 4, tel: (+48-12) 430 55 07, fax: (+48-12) 430 55 40, e-mail: biuro@akie.pl
Three apartments offering accommodation for 10 people at attractive prices (2 rooms with bathroom – 35 EUR).

ALEF HOTEL
ul. Szeroka 17, tel: (+48-12) 421 38 70, e-mail: alef@alef.pl, http://www.alef.pl
Located in the very heart of Kazimierz, the hotel offers enchanting spacious rooms with the atmosphere of the old days. The large rooms with a view of ul. Szeroka can accommodate up to 14 people. In high season rates (including breakfast) range from 70 EUR for a single and 88 EUR for a double. If you have the chance, ask for room no. 20 or 30 – these are the most beautiful rooms in this lovely place. The restaurant on the ground floor hosts live Jewish music concerts every day.

HOTEL ROOMS AT THE EL-JOT ART AND CONFERENCE CENTRE
ul. Miodowa 15, tel./fax: (+48-12) 421 33 26
e-mail: centrum@eljotcenter.pl, http://www.eljotcenter.pl
Stylish and cosy rooms, equipped with a bathroom, satellite TV, radio, telephone and access to the Internet. The centre organises conferences and can accommodate up to 30 persons. The SCENA EL-JOT Theatre situated in the same building can satisfy your spiritual needs. In peak season, the centre charges 239 zł/single, 299 zł/double, at weekends 219 zł and 279 zł respectively. Price includes breakfast; groups can negotiate the price.

KLEZMER-HOIS HOTEL
ul. Szeroka 6, tel./fax: (+48-12) 411 12 45, 411 16 22
e-mail: klezmer-hois@klezmer-hois.cracow.pl, http://www.klezmer.pl, http://www.klezmerhois.pl
Located in the building of the former Great Mikvah, a ritual bath house, the hotel offers 11 rooms and suites which can accommodate about 30 people. There are stylish and cosy rooms, as well as an excellent restaurant hosting concerts by Leopold Kozłowski, and other Jewish music concerts, which will provide unforgettable memories of your stay in Kazimierz. In peak season, the hotel charges 65 USD/single, 80 USD/double, 125 USD/suite. Prices include breakfast.

TOURNET GUEST ROOMS
ul. Miodowa 7, tel: (+48-12) 292 00 88, fax: (+48-12) 292 00 89
e-mail: tournet@accommodation.krakow.pl
http://www.nocleg.krakow.pl, http://www.accommodation.krakow.pl
Lovely rooms in various colours, equipped with a bathroom, TV, alarm clock, as well as a kettle, plates, cutlery and mugs, and tea and coffee free of charge. The rooms offer accommodation for 23 people. In high season the rates range from 33 EUR/single, 42 EUR/double, 52 EUR/triple. There are also two rooms of lower standards (24 EUR). Groups receive a 10% discount, and children under 12 stay free of charge. Prices include breakfast, which can be eaten in your own room.

LOREN GUEST ROOMS
ul. Krakowska 7, tel./fax: (+48-12) 292 22 11, http://www.infhotel.pl/krakow/loren
Comfortable rooms with bathrooms, situated on the fourth floor, offering accommodation for 26 people. The rates are 70 zł/single, other rooms 50 zł/person, 10-person-room – 40 zł/person; breakfast – 8 zł. These attractive prices will certainly catch students' attention.

KCD HOTEL
(National Counselling Department Kraków Training Centre),
ul. Meiselsa 1, tel: (+48-12) 424 05 55, 424 05 58, fax: (+48-12) 424 05 53,
e-mail:rezerwacja@noclegwkrakowie.pl, http://www.noclegwkrakowie.pl
The hotel offers 20 rooms (50 persons) of five standards, including rooms with fully-equipped kitchen and a bathroom; rooms with a bathroom; rooms with a shower but no toilet; or rooms without a bathroom. Rates range from 45 zł/person in triples (without a bathroom), through 120 zł/single with a kitchen to 150 zł/double with a bathroom. An exceptional offer in Kraków's Kazimierz.

NAD MŁYNKIEM GUEST ROOMS
pl. Wolnica 7, tel: (+48-12) 430 61 00
email: reservation@nadmlynkiem.krakow.pl, http://www.nadmlynkiem.krakow.pl
Cosy rooms above the stylish Młynek Café are equipped with a bathroom, TV and radio. Continental breakfast and vegetarian cuisine are served in the charming Młynek Café and gallery. The rates range from 25 EUR/single, 37 EUR/double, 56 EUR/triple to 75 EUR for a four-person suite, and 10 EUR/each additional person. Groups receive a discount up to 15%. Prices include breakfast, which can be eaten in your own room.

VOYAGE GUEST ROOMS
ul. Szeroka 7/8, tel: (+48-12) 431 04 51, fax: (+48-12) 431 04 42,
e-mail: info@voyage.travel.pl, http://www.voyage.travel.pl
Above an intense orange café there are 12 comfortable rooms with bathrooms: singles (33 EUR), doubles (43 EUR) and triples (53 EUR), offering accommodation for 30 people.

CULINARY DELIGHTS

In recent years, Kazimierz has become crowded with places offering culinary delights. Since there are nearly a hundred of them, the descriptions have been reduced to a minimum. For convenient reference the restaurants are arranged in alphabetical order.

RESTAURANTS

ALEF
ul. Szeroka 17, tel: (+48-12) 421 38 70, http://www.alef.pl
In these pre-war interiors, accompanied by daily live Jewish music and a unique atmosphere, you can try *gefilte* fish, *cholent* or Jewish caviar at moderate prices.

ANATEWKA
ul. Szeroka 3, tel: (+48-12) 431 01 29
A picturesque interior with live violinist and accordionist accompaniment to Polish and Jewish cuisine at reasonable prices: breakfast 9 zł, soups starting at 6 zł, salmon à la Leipzig is 29 zł; and a pint of beer is 6 zł.

ARIEL
ul. Szeroka 18, tel: (+48-12) 421 79 20
This lovely venue – a restaurant, gallery and café in one – hosts regular live concerts and serves delicious Jewish cuisine, rounded off with Polish and Russian cuisine. The chef's specialties are Sephardic style carp, Berdytchov soup and turkey tripe pot à la Dukla. The four rooms can accommodate up to 150 people.

ARKA NOEGO
ul. Szeroka 2, tel: (+48-12) 429 15 28
This cosy restaurant offers Jewish cuisine (chicken soup with matzo balls or *cholent*) at reasonable prices, accompanied by Israeli wine and live klezmer music concerts at weekends.

ART DES CREPES (WARSZTAT DOBREGO SMAKU) [GOOD TASTE WORKSHOP]
ul. Bożego Ciała 1, mobile: +48 506 148 597
Delicious crêpes made in front of your very eyes, from exclusively natural ingredients.

ASTORIA
ul. Józefa 24, tel: (+48-12) 432 50 10
This newly-opened restaurant at the Astoria hotel serves Polish cuisine at moderate prices. The chef's speciality is 'devil's ribs'.

BRASSERIE
ul. Gazowa 4, tel: (+48-12) 292 19 98
A former tram depot with a Parisian atmosphere, offering French cuisine at affordable prices: appetisers from 9 to 19 zł, main course (*crême brûlé* or *cordon bleu* chops) from 18 to 37 zł. Wine prices range from 59 zł to 219 zł. The restaurant can accommodate 90 people; there is a bathroom for disabled guests.

DONG A
ul. Miodowa 7, tel: (+48-12) 429 13 39
This small restaurant offers Chinese and Vietnamese cuisine at low prices (10-12 zł per meal).

GALICJA
ul. Starowiślna 71, tel: (+48-12) 429 26 07, http://www.galicja.com

This restaurant offers old Polish-style cuisine and, for an exclusive treat, venison. The chef's specialities are venison fillets with mushrooms in a creamy sauce, roe deer steaks in bacon and wild boar cutlets on toast.

FABRYKA PIZZY
ul. Józefa 34, tel: (+48-12) 433 80 80

This newly-opened restaurant serves an extensive selection of pizza (from 8.40 zł), pasta (from 9.60 zł), gnocchi (from 11.90 zł), soups, salads and 'bombers', that is, pizza rolls. All this and a modern, industrial interior decorated with steel cogs and other parts of machines.

GRILL-BAR MAREDO
ul. Dietla 33, entrance at ul. Augustiańska, tel: (+48-12) 429 55 24

Grilled dishes, as well as homemade dumplings. All dishes are made on the spot. A large beer costs 5 zł.

HOAN-KIEM
ul. Starowiślna 46, tel: (+48-12) 429 47 83

Chinese-Vietnamese cuisine at attractive prices.

KLEZMER-HOIS
ul. Szeroka 6, tel: (+48-12) 411 12 45, http://www.klezmer.pl

Delicious Jewish cuisine served in an enchanting interior. Stuffed goose necks, *cholent*, *kugel* or *latkes* with apple sauce, not to mention 'Leopold's Set'. Prices range from 11 to 36 zł for a main course.

KLIMAT
pl. Wolnica 7, tel: (+48-12) 422 00 46

This restaurant serves old Polish cuisine, such as Krak's snack (stuffed chicken) or Janeczka's cheesecake served hot. A large beer – 5 zł.

KUCHNIA I WINO
ul. Józefa 13, tel: (+48-12) 421 77 36

The restaurant of Izabela Różycka, the winner of the 1st International Soup Festival, offering French cuisine, and fresh seafood served on Thursday and Friday. Moreover, there is an extensive selection of top shelf French wine and an enchanting atmosphere (however, check the mineral water price before you order).

NAVARRA
ul. Podbrzezie 2, tel: (+48-12) 431 19 42

This tiny restaurant serves delicious Mexican dishes and Jewish bagels with various toppings (2-9.50 zł).

RESTAURACJA NORYMBERSKA
ul. Krakowska 27, tel: (+48-12) 422 42 51

Nuremberg cuisine in a pleasant interior. Prices range from 12 zł (regular dinner) to 52 zł (Bavarian set for two). The traditional Nuremberg set is lentil soup, roast in gingerbread sauce, *spatzle*, obatzer cheese and a Nuremberg pretzel.

PIZZERIA BANOLLI
pl. Wolnica 10, tel: (+48-12) 432 11 22, 423 00 00, http://www.banolli.pl

A rich selection of pizzas in terms of taste, size and price: a medium pizza (28 cm) is about 10 zł, the largest – the big party pizza (41 cm) – 25 zł. The pizzeria accepts Internet orders and offers pizza deliveries.

PIWNICE REGENTA
ul. Bożego Ciała 19, tel: (+48-12) 430 62 11
In the quiet, cosy cellars of the Regent Hotel this restaurant offers Polish cuisine alongside a wide selection of wine.

POLAKOWSKI 1899
ul. Miodowa 39, tel: (+48-12) 421 07 76
This small self-service restaurant offers Polish and Jewish cuisine, especially convenient when you are in a hurry. The price range varies somewhat – every day features a different *plat du jour*.

RAJ UTRACONY
ul. Meiselsa 11, tel: (+48-12) 430 64 83
This tiny, recently-opened restaurant serves Polish cuisine with emphasis on Western Galicia cuisine (pan-fried hearts, and the host's special cutlet) at reasonable prices.

STOLARNIA
ul. Józefa 14, tel: (+48-12) 430 68 66, http://www.stolarniakrakow.republika.pl/index6.htm
This 'grill-bar-gallery' in one serves grilled, fried and roasted dishes and various salads at reasonable prices. It hosts affordable private parties and is open to various forms of art.

STUDNIA ŻYCZEŃ
pl. Nowy 6, tel: (+48-12) 629 53 37
This restaurant boasts an interesting interior and Italian dishes: filling soups, spaghetti (10 – 16 zł) and pizza (12 – 20 zł). Spaghetti in 4 cheese sauce is quite popular here. A glass of wine (Hungarian Egri Bikaver) is 5 zł, and a large beer 5.50 zł.

SZEROKA NO. 1
ul. Szeroka 1, tel: (+48-12) 421 07 76
A stylish restaurant in former Jewish shops, offering mainly Jewish-style cuisine: onion soup with caramel (7 zł), or *cholent* (16 zł). A large draught beer for 6 zł. The turquoise walls and antique furniture create an enchanting atmosphere.

TRATTORIA
ul. Brzozowa 18, tel: (+48-12) 292 33 17
Italian cuisine: lasagne, spaghetti or pasta (13 – 25 zł), and delicious pizza (*carne bianca* with crab and mayonnaise is worth trying – 18.50 zł). A large beer costs 4.70 zł.

U VINCENTA
ul. Józefa 11, tel: (+48-12) 430 68 34
The only dumpling (*pierogi*) restaurant in Kazimierz – a selection of 25 kinds of dumplings: with meat, cheese, vegetarian, fruit and sweet fillings. Especially recommended are dumplings with cheese and walnut filling (6.50 zł) or smoked fish and feta cheese. Special offers: Monday – meat dumpling day with beet root soup (*barszcz*) free, Wednesday – surprise dumpling day, Saturday – vegetarian dumpling day with sour milk (*kefir*) as a bonus. This tiny, cosy bar's interior was inspired by Vincent van Gogh. The orange walls, green tables and chairs, and ceramic accessories with sunflower motifs create a cheerful atmosphere for the interior.

FAST FOOD

Almost every day a new place opens in Kazimierz offering cheap and fast food. Often they are tiny, cosy places where you can have a nice meal without blowing your budget.

The round building in the middle of **PLAC NOWY** hosts four bars: **ENDZIOR**, **NAMAXA**, **U DANUSI** and **BAR OKO**, where you can have a *zapiekanka* [a toasted baguette with mushrooms and cheese, especially recommended with chives at Namaxa], hamburgers or lunch for just a few zlotys. The **MINI BAR** in ul. Miodowa offers a similar menu. At night you can satisfy your hunger at **GRILL NA KAZIMIERZU** opposite ul. Meiselsa and the cult shop **PIERSIÓWECZKA I FAJECZKA** [Hip Flask and Pipe], where you can get alcohol and cigarettes. Moreover, you can still find some typical communist 'milk bars' serving cheap food, if you feel like trying what it was like back then: **BAR MLECZNY POD FILARKAMI**, **BAR SYRENA** in ul. Starowiślna, **BAR KAZIMIERZ**, **SZYBKI KĘS** in ul. Krakowska and **BAR MACIUŚ** in ul. Dietla.

RESTAURACYJKA BIDA Z NĘDZĄ
ul. Meiselsa 14, tel: (+48-12) 292 04 54
Every day one dish is served for 10 zł.
BISTRO POD 13
ul. Miodowa 13, tel: (+48-12) 656 48 50
In a sense this is a cult bar – you can order delicious homemade food for very little money.
JADŁODAJNIA CZERWONE JABŁUSZKO
ul. Krakowska 7, tel: (+48-12) 431 13 37
Tasty homemade food; lunch set of the day for 9.90 zł, plus chicken soup with noodles free. Soups from 2.90 zł, main course à la carte – 13.90 zł.
JADŁODAJNIA POD ZŁOTĄ RYBKĄ
ul. Meiselsa 2B (at the corner of ul. Augustiańska), tel: (+48-12) 422 20 96
Open from Monday to Friday, this restaurant serves 'fish with class and other delicious food'; a wide selection of fish (8-15 zł).
RESTAURACJA U DOROTY
ul. Miodowa 25
Polish cuisine at low prices – a wide selection of dumplings for 5 zł (10 per portion).
EMILPOL
pl. Wolnica 13
This interesting bar offers delicious lunches and snacks at very reasonable prices.
MR KOTLET
ul. Dajwór 25, tel: (+48-12) 432 93 00, 432 93 01
An extensive selection of chops and cutlets (devil, Genoa, stuffed with mushrooms, etc.) at attractive prices. Sets from 9.90 zł.
OD ZMIERZCHU DO ŚWITU
ul. św. Sebastiana 33
A pleasant bar, open 21 hours a day (9 am to 6 am), serving Polish cuisine at low prices.

PUBS AND CAFÉS THAT ALSO SERVE FOOD

CAFÉ MŁYNEK
pl. Wolnica 7, tel: (+48-12) 430 62 02
This tiny, cosy café-bar with warm lighting and mood jazz or Latin American music, photos of Marlene Dietrich and Marilyn Monroe on the walls, decorated with coffee grinders and cof-

fee machines, serves vegetarian cuisine: quiche, homemade dumplings, stuffed cabbage rolls in mushroom sauce, and so on, at reasonable prices. A large beer – 5 zł, Beamish. Numerous concerts and exhibitions.

CAFÉ HAMLET
ul. Miodowa 9, tel: (+48-12) 422 12 11
In this pleasant interior you can have homemade dumplings, plus excellent cheese or onion soup at affordable prices.

KOLANKO NO. 6
ul. Józefa 17, tel: (+48-12) 292 03 20
This lovely pub is renowned for its extensive selection of pancakes at very attractive prices (from 7 zł for two pancakes), with spinach and feta cheese, Mexican or broccoli stuffing. The onion soup with cheese and toast is also worth trying.

MOMO
ul. Dietla 49, mobile.: 609 685 775
Healthy, inexpensive, ecological food made without meat, fish, or eggs (no microwaves), inspired by world cuisine. A paradise for vegetarians and vegans.

PROCES PARZENIA KAFKI
ul. Podbrzezie 2, tel: (+48-12) 429 13 10
This small pub offers various kinds of coffee, delicious *cholent*, lasagna, spaghetti, pancakes and salads at reasonable prices. A large beer – 5 zł.

SZEROKA NO 1
ul. Szeroka 1, tel: (+48-12) 421 07 76 (see p. 149)

CAFÉS, PUBS

Kazimierz is crammed with pubs, cafés and clubs. Some have been here for years, others come and go. Prominent figures from contemporary artistic circles often settle here in Kazimierz, open a pub or a gallery, and stay for good.

Your visit to Kazimierz will not be complete unless you visit one of the local pubs, have a beer or an intriguing cocktail, sit down for a while and absorb the atmosphere of this unique town. For some recommendations on places with atmosphere, have a look at Route 5, *Retracing Bohemian Kazimierz*.

8 DZIEŃ TYGODNIA
ul. Podbrzezie 4
With both an unforgettable atmosphere and name [The Eighth Day of the Week], this wide bar is shaped like a boat, and is a place where you can always find some company and read newspapers. Affordable prices.

ALCHEMIA
ul. Estery 5, tel: (+48-12) 421 22 00, http://www.alchemia.com.pl
A cult pub in Kazimierz, where you can meet interesting people and have a great time. The dark interiors are filled with the atmosphere of the old days and attract crowds. The venue is popular with Kraków bohemian circles as it is open late into the night, has a stage and a small cinema, and hosts numerous artistic (theatre, music and film) events.

ALOHA
ul. Miodowa 28a

Being here feels like a holiday in Hawaii: Hawaiian music, beach chairs and dancing.

ANTIDOTUM
ul. Estery 5, tel: (+48-12) 431 93 90

This pleasant, cosy pub offers a wide selection of tea and concerts.

ANTYKVARIAT
ul. Dietla 75, tel: (+48-12) 429 27 50, http://www.klubantykwariat.pl

In this club you can listen to drum'n'bass and house, have something to eat, drink a 'rabid dog' for a few zlotys or a large beer for 6 zł. Wednesday and weekends feature live parties.

BARAKA
ul. Warszauera 1 (corner of ul. Warszauera and Plac Nowy)

This newly-opened pub with its futuristic interior differs from other Kazimierz pubs: the walls and floor are covered with a motif of blue circles and the couches are covered with red material.

CAFÉ BERBERYS
pl. Wolnica 13, tel: (+48-12) 292 04 95

Situated off the beaten track, this cosy café offers cocktails, such as 'Angel's Smile'.

CAFÉ HAMLET
ul. Miodowa 9, tel: (+48-12) 422 12 11 (see p. 151)

CAFÉ MŁYNEK
pl. Wolnica 7, tel: (+48-12) 430 62 02 (see p. 150)

DRUKARNIA NA KAZIMIERZU
pl. Nowy 8, tel: (+48-12) 421 3231

A bright and contemporary interior which calls a student club to mind. Numerous concerts (Wed., Thu.) and dance parties (Sat., Sun.).

ESZEWERIA
ul. Józefa 9, tel: (+48-12) 292 04 59

In this enchanting interior, with its unique atmosphere and antique furniture, you can have a beer (5 zł), various types of tea served in teapots, dumplings or just sit and relax in this wonderful cosy place. Mulled wine with herbs and fruit, ice drinks in summer in the backyard. A must.

KAWA POD KOGUTKIEM
ul. Józefa 11, tel: (+48-12) 430 65 32

This lovely, tiny coffee shop offers an extensive selection of coffee, but sells no alcohol and plays no music.

KAWIARNIA NAUKOWA
ul. Jakuba 29, tel: (+48-12) 421 53 83

In this café's unusual interior, concerts and philosophical lectures take place. A large beer at 5 zł, cocktails between 6.50-16 zł.

KOLANKO NO. 6
ul. Józefa 17, tel: (+48-12) 292 03 20 (see p. 133)

KRAINA SZEPTÓW
ul. Izaaka 1/1, tel: (+48-12) 292 09 49

An interesting interior with a bell hanging from the ceiling. Recently the pub has expanded to the first floor, taking over the former Pub Na Piętrze.

KRÓLICZE OCZY
ul. Estery 14, tel: (+48-12) 431 10 31
A very cosy and charming place decorated with photographs with red 'rabbit eyes'. Standard prices; funk, jazz and black metal.

KURIOZUM
ul. Józefa 25, tel: (+48-12) 421 51 34, http://www.kuriozum.com
A sleepy café with a crimson upstairs, and an underground rock pub downstairs.

LA HABANA
ul. Miodowa 22, mobile: 602 192 582
This warm Cuban pub offers delicious *corne picada con frijoces* (at 8 zł), Cuban cigars, beer cocktails, and cocktails designed by Hemingway.

LE PIANKA
ul. Szeroka 10, tel: (+48-12) 423 08 74
Chaotic aesthetics, Aztec decor, Chinese straws, modern furniture and loud music.

LES COULEURS
ul. Estery 10, tel: (+48-12) 429 42 70
A reminiscence of France in Kazimierz – to the accompaniment of French music, you can try French cuisine snacks, read some French press, celebrate French festivals or have incredible cocktails. This café opens first in Kazimierz (at 7 am). The owner is the founder of the International Soup Festival.

LOKATOR
ul. Krakowska 10 (entrance from ul. Meiselsa), tel: (+48-12) 422 25 53
http://www.lokator.pointblue.com.pl
A café, gallery and pub that offers unusual cocktails: 'Tenant', 'Neighbours', as well as chimerical chocolate with whipped cream. It also hosts various exhibitions, from drawings to photographs.

LUFA
ul. Wąska 2, tel: (+48-12) 429 67 74
A newly-opened pub with a modern interior highlighted with orange light.

MEHANOFF
ul. Estery 8, mobile: 609 049 873
An intriguing interior, theme parties, acid jazz, folk music, and standard prices.

MLECZARNIA
ul. Meiselsa 20, tel: (+48-12) 421 85 32, http://www.figiel.l.pl
An extremely cosy café with old-fashioned purple walls, lace tablecloths, antiques and old photos. Opposite the café in the courtyard between Meiselsa and Józefa Streets spreads a magical open-air café in the summer. A wide selection of coffee, delicious hot chocolate, draught beer (5.50 zł), sweet specialties, such as apple in caramel (4 zł) and walnut cake (4.50 zł).

OPIUM
ul. Jakuba 19, tel: (+48-12) 421 94 61
A modern pub with an open-air mezzanine, providing a view of the Jewish cemetery. Hosts concerts and dance parties at weekends.

OSMOZA
ul. Józefa 18
A newly-opened pub in a long, typically Kazimierz interior, full of aspiration and enthusiasm. Jazz concerts on Thursday and Saturday.

PORTOFINO
ul. Wąska 2, tel: (+48-12) 431 05 37
A recently-opened stylish café and pub in crimson and green.

POZYTYWKA
ul. Bożego Ciała 12, tel: (+48-12) 430 64 82
A club, pub and gallery in one, set in a modern interior that is not very Kazimierz in style. Access to the Internet at every table, club music, interesting exhibitions.

PROCES PARZENIA KAFKI
ul. Podbrzezie 2, tel: (+48-12) 429 13 10 (see p. 151)

PROPAGANDA
ul. Podbrzezie 20
A socialist museum of propaganda, full of theme items, resembling granddad's attic. Cocktails include the 'Retreat from Moscow' or 'Fidel's smile'.

PRZERWA
ul. Mostowa 2
A newly-opened club off the beaten pub track, i.e. ul. Szeroka and Plac Nowy.

PTASZYL
ul. Szeroka 10, tel: (+48-12) 429 65 67
An intensely coloured interior with tree branches for the 'birdos' hanging from the ceiling. Modern music, often modern jazz. Fireplace in winter, tables outside in ul. Szeroka in summer. Standard prices.

RAMÓWKA
ul. Podbrzezie 5, tel: (+48-12) 422 82 13
The most extensive selection of coffee in Kazimierz, served in a tiny, cosy café with a mezzanine, decorated with picture frames. Plans for the future: exhibitions.

SAN SEBASTIAN
ul. Dietla 75/3 (entrance in ul. św. Sebastiana)
Offers coffee and morning papers or a romantic candlelit dinner in its elegant interior.

SARA
ul. Meiselsa 17, tel: (+48-12) 430 64 49
This tiny café at the Center for Jewish Culture has heart, which is evident in each coffee or cake.

SINGER
ul. Estery 22, tel: (+48-12) 292 06 22
This cult pub is the oldest in Kazimierz, and uses 'Singer' sewing-machines as tables. The interior is filled with Kazimierz atmosphere. The pub is extremely popular with Kraków bohemian circles, and is open late into the night. A must.

STAJNIA
ul. Józefa 12, tel: (+48-12) 423 72 02
This pub is located in former horse stables. In summer it occupies the loveliest courtyard in Kazimierz, and hosts concerts and dance parties with Latin American music.

TABOO
ul. Szeroka 10, tel: (+48-12) 421 73 89, http://www.amnesty.krakow.pl/lgbt
Hidden away in cellars, this night club is open from 6 pm to 4 am, and features DJs and parties.

TAJEMNICZY OGRÓD NA KAZIMIERZU
pl. Nowy 9

An interesting interior, theme parties, standard prices (beer – 5.50 zł).

TAROT
pl. Nowy 9

A newly-opened and mysterious pub with a genuine fortune-teller and its own Tarot currency.

TRANSYLWANIA
ul. Szeroka 9, tel: (+48-12) 431 14 09

A theme pub with a friendly atmosphere, vampire decor, blood-drinking secrets, spontaneous parties and things to eat. Plenty of garlic on the walls, giving you the illusion of security.

UCHO VAN GOGHA
ul. Brzozowa 4, tel: (+48-12) 421 96 89, http://www.uchoangogha.w.interia.pl

Sunny cellars lifted from van Gogh paintings, offering drinks and good fun, plus complimentary jacket potatoes.

ULICA KROKODYLI
ul. Szeroka 30, tel: (+48-12) 431 05 16

This pub styled to resemble ul. Krokodyli from Bruno Schulz's story offers the 'Crocodile tears' cocktail and pop music. In summer: open-air cafés in Szeroka and Ciemna Streets.

VOYAGE
ul. Szeroka 7/8

An intense orange interior with wicker chairs, and open-air café in ul. Szeroka.

WARSZTAT
ul. Izaaka 3, tel: (+48-12) 292 09 09, http://www.warsztat.krakow.pl

An intriguing 'shelter house' for instruments and a place where you can tune your internal spiritual 'instrument'. Mood interior, candlelight, a grand piano bar and the piano in the corner is not a prop. Draught beer (5.50 zł) and delicious walnut cake (4 zł).

WYSYPISKO
ul. Podbrzezie 2, tel: (+48-12) 421 99 29

With an interior that resembles a garbage tip, this pub offers numerous attractions (discounts for women: the price of beer goes down with every 10th beer), and unconventional exhibitions.

YE OLDE GOAT
ul. Ciemna 15, tel: (+48-12) 430 65 65, http://www.hoteleden.pl

These 16th-century cellars host a secluded bar with draught beer (4.99 zł) and top shelf alcohols. Every Thursday you are more than welcome to have a go at karaoke.

GALLERIES

As already mentioned, Kazimierz has become an artistic enclave where numerous galleries are centred, promoting contemporary art and young artists. More and more venues have joined the 'Thursdays in Kazimierz' project. Every first Thursday of the month is a big day for Kazimierz galleries: exhibition launches are held, galleries are open late, and lots of people meet. It is worth popping in here.

GALERIE D'ART NAÏF
ul. Józefa 11, tel: (+48-12) 421 06 37, e-mail: galeria@artnaive.sky.pl, http://www.artnaive.sky.pl

This gallery boasts the largest private collection of art naïf, non-professional art or *l'art brut*. Detached from official trends, it has impressed those who have devoted a bit of attention to it. The gallery promotes both mature artists (Nikifor, Ociepka, Heródek, etc.) and debutants.

THE LABIRYNT GALLERY
ul. Józefa 15, tel: (+48-12) 292 13 00, e-mail: labirynt@and.pl, http://www.galerialabirynt.and.pl
This gallery presents contemporary art and promotes debutant artists. It displays painting, graphics, sculpture and applied art, and hosts numerous group and individual exhibitions. It has cooperated with various art organizations and participates in numerous projects, including 'Thursdays in Kazimierz'.

THE NOVA GALLERY
ul. Józefa 22 (entrance from ul. Nowa), tel: (+48-12) 292 10 42
e-mail: galeria@nova.art.pl, http://www.nova.art.pl
This gallery presents and promotes young contemporary Polish art, with emphasis on art closely bound with reality and giving direct commentary. Conceptual art strongly related to the human and object is appreciated here. Apart from mature artists, it presents a wide range of art forms: from hyperrealism, photorealism to pop-realism by artists of the young generation.

THE OLYMPIA GALLERY
ul. Estery 16, tel: (+48-12) 429 37 34, e-mail: sklep@olympiagaleria.pl, http://www.olympiagaleria.pl
This gallery promotes young artists, mainly from Kraków. The gallery also hosts artistic dialogues and meetings, and presents paintings, graphics and applied art.

THE OTWARTA PRACOWNIA GALLERY
ul. Dietla 11, tel: (+48-12) 636 71 98
An entirely independent, non-commercial gallery situated on the outskirts of old Kazimierz, open only on Friday 6 pm – 8 pm or by appointment. Although the gallery presents all aspects of contemporary art, it puts an emphasis on the role of image in the multi-media era.

THE RAVEN GALLERY
ul. Brzozowa 7, tel: (+48-12) 431 11 29
e-mail: galeria@raven.krakow.pl, http://www.raven.krakow.pl
This gallery presents drawing, paintings, graphics, and applied art, with a special emphasis on art déco furniture. Contemporary art exhibitions are held here, but you can also find 19th-century *École de Paris* or Kraków Group works of art.

THE SZALOM GALLERY
ul. Józefa 16, tel: (+48-12) 292 32 70, 430 65 05
e-mail: artszalom@poczta.wp.pl, http://www.kazimierz.com/artszalom
This gallery aims at preserving the world of Jewish culture existing here before the Second World War, as well as staging various exhibitions. The gallery owners desire to create a 'friendly' gallery for people not necessarily associated with art, to promote the work of their friends and of others: numerous artists of *Piwnica pod Baranami*, *Loch Camelot* cabaret musicians, singers and writers.

THE OTHER WAY GALLERY
ul. Józefa 26, tel: (+48-12) 426 93 40
e-mail: galeria@theotherway.com.pl, http://www.theotherway.com.pl
One of the youngest Kazimierz galleries, The Other Way puts an emphasis on interior design and art promotion. It assembles artists, painters, illustrators, graphic designers, sculptors, as well as glass, ceramics, amber and wood artists, who would like to assist us in designing our dream interior.

THEATRES

THE SCENA EL-JOT THEATRE
ul. Miodowa 15, tel: (+48-12) 430 66 06, e-mail: teatr@eljot.art.pl, http://www.eljot.art.pl
"This intimate theatre of gesture, word, and musical harmony; a theatre of poetic realism and metaphysical metaphors", run by Jadwiga Leśniak-Jankowska, presents intriguing musical shows, concerts and musical poems. Tickets: 20 zł, students: 15 zł,

MUSEUMS

THE SEWERYN UDZIELA ETHNOGRAPHICAL MUSEUM
Permanent exhibition "Polish Folk Culture" – pl. Wolnica 1, the former Kazimierz town hall
Temporary exhibitions – ul. Krakowska 46, "Dom Esterki"
tel: (+48-12) 430 55 63, 430 55 75, fax: 430 63 30
e-mail: mek@tele2.pl, http://www.mek.tele2.pl
Open: Mon. 10 am – 6 pm, Tues. – closed, Wed.-Fri. 10 am – 3 pm, Sat.-Sun. 10 am – 2 pm, summertime every day 10 am – 5 pm except Tues. (closed) and Sun. (10 am – 2 pm). Tickets: 6 zł, students: 4 zł, filming and photographing charge: 20 zł.
The museum presents the oldest and most valuable Polish ethnographical collection. In this former town hall, you can see models of regional folk huts, chambers, workshops, costumes, jewellery, and musical instruments, and learn about crafts and folk art, customs and other aspects of life. Temporary exhibitions focus on other cultures or particular themes, e.g. the history of the Christmas tree or Hindu dolls.

CITY ENGINEERING MUSEUM OF KRAKÓW
ul. św. Wawrzyca 15, tel./fax: 421 12 42
e-mail: museum@mimk.com.pl, http://www.mimk.com.pl
Open every day (except Mon.) 10 am – 4 pm. Tickets: 5 zł, students: 3 zł (Tues. – free admission); educational interactive exhibition: 3 zł.
The museum's collection illustrates the development of Kraków's public transport, power station, gas-works, and displays old trams, a horse-drawn omnibus or summer horse-drawn tram, and about 30 historical car and motorcycle models. Temporary exhibitions on particular themes (*Talking Machines: Phonograph – Gramophone*, *Kraków City Gas-Works 1856-1950*), and art (*Angels – Christoph Krane's Birds or Sculptures*).

THE HISTORICAL MUSEUM OF THE CITY OF KRAKÓW. Branch: THE HISTORY AND CULTURE OF JEWS
Stara Synagoga, ul. Szeroka 24, tel: (+48-12) 422 09 62
Open April-Oct.: Mon. 10 am – 2 pm, Tues. – Sun. 10 am – 5 pm, Oct.-April every day (except Tues.) 9 am – 3:30 pm. Tickets: 6 zł, students: 4 zł, groups: 4 zł and 3 zł respectively. Permanent exhibition on the Kraków Jews' traditions, history and culture. Temporary theme exhibitions (see Route 1).

SYNAGOGUES

THE ISAAC SYNAGOGUE
ul. Kupa 18, tel: (+48-12) 430 55 77

Open every day (except Sat. and Jewish holidays) 9 am – 7 pm, tickets: 7 zł, students: 6 zł
Documentary films: *The Jewish District of Kazimierz* (1936) and *The Removal to the Cracow Ghetto* (1941) as well as other war-time films shown alongside the entitled *In Memory of Polish Jews* exhibition.

THE REMUH SYNAGOGUE
ul. Szeroka 40; open Mon.-Fri. Sun.9 am – 4 pm, tickets: 5 zł, students: 2 zł
The only Orthodox synagogue offering regular religious services, adjacent to the oldest preserved Jewish cemetery in Kraków.

THE TEMPEL SYNAGOGUE
ul. Miodowa 24; open Mon.- Fri., Sun. 9 am – 4 pm, tickets: 5 zł, students: 2 zł
The only Reform synagogue in Kraków.

NEW CEMETERY, ul. Miodowa
Open every day (except Sat. and Jewish holidays) 9 am – 5 pm, admission free.

CHURCHES

THE CORPUS CHRISTI CHURCH, ul. Bożego Ciała
Visiting not allowed during services, admission free.

ST CATHERINE AND ST MARGARET'S CHURCH, ul. Augustiańska
Open Tues.-Sat. 9 am – 1 pm, Sun. 2 pm – 5 pm, closed Mon. and the last Sat. and Sun. of the month, entrance from ul. Skałeczna, admission free.

THE ST MICHAEL THE ARCHANGEL AND ST STANISLAUS THE BISHOP MARTYR CHURCH, ul. Skałeczna
Visiting not allowed during services, admission free.

THE MOST HOLY TRINITY CHURCH, ul. Krakowska
Visiting not allowed during services, admission free.

OTHER

POST OFFICE
ul. Starowiślna 56/50, Mon. – Fri. 8 am – 8 pm
Postal service, pl. Nowy, Mon. – Fri. 8 am – 6 pm, Sat. 8 am – noon

INTERNET CAFÉS
ul. Miodowa 26, open: 9 am – 10 pm (3 zł/h)
ul. Józefa 15, open: 10 am – 10 pm (2 zł/h, 1.50 zł/30 mins)

BANKS
BANK POLSKIEJ SPÓŁDZIELCZOŚCI SA, ul. Bożego Ciała 23, tel: (+48-12) 430 68 40
DEUTSCHE BANK, ul. Starowiślna 88
KREDYT BANK, ul. Kupa 3, tel: (+48-12) 422 31 86, 422 86 22; ul. Dietla 68; ul. Miodowa 11
PEKAO SA I Branch, ul. Szeroka 22, tel: (+48-12) 421 80 87, fax: 421 65 25
III Branch, ul. Krakowska 46, tel: (+48-12) 421 95 90, fax: 421 92 17
PKO BP, pl. Wolnica 12a, tel: (+48-12) 431 09 47, 431 09 35

CASH MACHINES

Gospodarczy Bank Południowo-Zachodni SA, ul. Kupa 2
Bank Gospodarki Żywnościowej, ul. Krakowska 36
BPS SA, ul. Bożego Ciała 23
BPHPBK, ul. Dajwór 27
PEKAO SA, ul. Szeroka 22
KREDYT BANK, ul. Kupa 3
DEUTSCHE BANK, ul. Starowiślna 88

PHARMACIES

KRAKOWSKA, ul. Krakowska 35, tel: (+48-12) 656 18 54
NA KAZIMIERZU, ul. Krakowska 49, tel: (+48-12) 430 53 46
NA SKAŁCE, ul. Krakowska 19, tel: (+48-12) 292 05 76
NIEBIESKA, ul. Starowiślna 77, tel: (+48-12) 421 24 63
NIEBIESKA, plac Wolnica 12a/4, tel: (+48-12) 430 58 54
POD ŚW. HUBERTEM, ul. Krakowska 1, tel: (+48-12) 422 19 98
POD ESTERKĄ, ul. Estery 3

BICYCLE RENTAL

DWA KOŁA Bicycle Rental, ul. Józefa 5, open 9 am – 8:30 pm.
Nearly 100 Dutch bicycles on offer – city, mountain, adult and children's bicycles. Bicycle and ski service. Rental for the whole day costs 30 zł, 5 hours – 20 zł, 3 hours – 15 zł. Discounts for few day rentals.
The Bicycle Rental is run by the Aniela Salawa Foundation for Those Suffering from MS, established as part of a project by a Dutch consulting organization called Wesseling Groep.

'MUSTS'

JARDEN BOOKSHOP
ul. Szeroka 2, tel: (+48-12) 421 71 66, 429 13 74, http://www.jarden.pl;
Open Mon.–Fri. 10 am – 6 pm, Sat. – Sun. 10 am – 3 pm
This unique bookshop offers Jewish literature on history, philosophy, religion and culture, the Holocaust, belles-lettres, guidebooks, albums, souvenirs, tapes and CDs with Jewish music. In addition to being a bookstore, the place is also a tourist agency which does not charge much for 'live' and knowledgeable guides who can show you round Jewish Kazimierz and retrace *Schindler's List*.

GALICIA JEWISH MUSEUM – New!
ul. Dajwór 18, tel: (+48-12) 421 68 42
http:// www.galiciajewishmuseum.org
This freshly-opened Galicia Heritage Jewish Museum presents a unique exhibition entitled *Traces of Memory* – over 140 large format colour photographs taken from towns and villages in Polish Galicia that document traces of the Jewish past still visible in southern Poland. The museum also houses an impressive Jewish bookstore and a café.

CENTRE FOR JEWISH CULTURE

ul. Meiselsa 17, tel: (+48-12) 430 64 49, 430 64 52, http://www.judaica.pl

The Center has been involved in the promotion of Jewish culture in Kazimierz for 10 years now. *Beit Hadash – The Month of Encounters with Jewish Culture* has been organized since 1996, as well as various exhibitions, concerts, film showings, lectures and cultural dialogues. You can learn and see a lot.

UL. JÓZEFA

No visit to Kazimierz would be complete without a visit to ul. Józefa. It is a must – apart from the above-mentioned galleries – lovely shops and antique galleries, jewellery, souvenir and applied art shops, such as STARY SKLEP (no. 16) with its unique atmosphere; LAMUS GALERIA (no. 3); NASZE ATELIER (no. 14) with its splendid sculptured angels and Jews; YAKUZ GIFTS (no. 11) with its jewellery, angels and so on; BLAZKO KINDERY (no. 13) with its jewellery; ARS VITREA (no. 9) with its outstanding stained glass windows; and a number of antique shops (ANTYKI JÓZEFA, ANTYKI STAROCIE, STAROCIE, SZTUKATERIA).

You definitely should pay a visit to ul. Brzozowa with the PURsicZAN GALLERY and ART KOMIS, as well as to ul. Krakowska 13 to the HURTOWNIA RZECZY ŁADNYCH, where you can buy absolutely fantastic souvenirs. Music lovers should pop into a cosy second-hand shop called HIGH FIDELITY at ul. Podbrzezie 6, with an impressive vinyl and CD collection.

PLAC NOWY

Market days at plac Nowy: Mon.– Sat.: fruit, vegetables and meat; Tues. and Fri.: fowl; Sat.: antique fair, flea market; Sun.: clothes fair.

YIDDISH – MINI PHRASE BOOK

As already mentioned, the Kraków Jews living in Kazimierz spoke mainly Yiddish. The origins of the Yiddish language date back to the 10th and 11th centuries when Jews settled along the Rhine in southern Germany. It consists of German vocabulary (around 70%), Hebrew (around 10%) and the remaining 20% of the vocabulary was adapted from Slavic languages. The alphabet is written in Hebrew from right to left. There is a quiet humour in Yiddish, and a large amount of vocabulary expressing emotions – like no other language in the world. Moreover, it is the language of the Jewish demons and *dybbuks* present in the stories of I.B. Singer, who wrote in this language and was awarded the Nobel Prize in 1981. It is worth learning a few basic expressions in this language in order to fully absorb the Kazimierz atmosphere. However, you can no longer hear this tongue in Kraków's Kazimierz.

א	(a,o)	alef	ח	kh	khes	ע	e	ayen
ב	b	beyz	ט	t	tes	פ	p	pey
ב	v	veyz	י	(y, i)	yud	פ	f	fey
ג	g	gimml	כ	k	kof	צ	c	tsaddik
ד	d	daled	ל	l	lamed	ק	k	kuf
ה	h	hey	מ	m	mem	ר	r	reysh
ו	u	vov	נ	n	nun	ש	sh	shin
ז	z	zayn	ס	s	samekh	ת	(s, t)	tov

Good morning	[sholem alejkhem]	שָׁלוֹם־עֲלֵיכֶם
Good morning	[alejkhem sholem]	עֲלֵיכֶם־שָׁלוֹם
or		
Good morning	[gut morgn]	גוט מאָרגן
Good morning	[gut yor]	גוט יאָר
Good evening	[gutn ovnt]	גוטן אָוונט
Good evening	[gut yor]	גוט יאָר
What's your name?	[vi heystu?]	ווי הייסטו?
What's your name, sir/madam?	[vi heyst ir?]	ווי הייסט איר?
My name is ...	[ikh heys...]	איך הייס...
How are you?	[vos makhstu?]	וואָס מאַכסטו?
How are you, sir/madam?	[vos makht ir?]	וואָס מאַכט איר?
What's up?	[vos hert zikh?]	וואָס הערט זיך?
All right.	[nishkoshe]	נישקשה
It could always be better.	[s'ken alemol zayn beser]	סʼקען אַלעמאָל זיַין רעסער
It could always be worse.	[s'ken alemol zayn erger]	סʼקען אַלעמאָל זיַין ערגער
Where are you from?	[fun vanet kumstu?]	פֿון וואַנעט קומסטו?
Where are you from, sir/madam?	[fun vanet kumt ir?]	פֿון וואַנעט קומט איר?
I come from Kraków.	[ikh kum fun kroke]	איך קום פֿון קראָקע
Good bye	[a gutn tog]	אַ גוטן טאָג
Good bye	[a gutn]	אַ גוטן
Good night	[a gute nakht]	אַ גוטע נאַכט
Good night	[a gut yor]	אַ גוט יאָר
Be well	[zay gezunt]	זיַי געזונט
Good luck/congratulations	[mazl tov]	מזל טוב!
Cheers	[lekhaim]	לחיים!

INDEX OF PLACES DESCRIBED IN *THE WALKING TOURS IN KAZIMIERZ*

QUESTIONNAIRE FOR OUR READERS

Dear Travellers,
We warmly invite you to join Klub Bezdrożnika [Off-the-Beaten-Track Travellers' Club]. Membership in the Club gives you the opportunity to purchase guidebooks, maps, atlases, phrase-books, travel books and multi-media publications more easily and at reduced prices. Klub Bezdrożnika has been established for you – people travelling round the world and seeking information useful for planning trips. All this information is at your fingertips – you can find it in the guidebooks published by Wydawnictwo Bezdroża and on the travel website **www.bezdroza.com**.

In order to become a member of the Club, you just need to **fill in this questionnaire** and send it to the Publisher's address.
Information about promotions and offers resulting from your membership in the Club is available on the website www.bezdroza.com.
If you wish to receive our newsletter via email, tick the appropriate box ☐.

YOUR TRAVELS

1. Which places have you visited already or do you plan to visit?:

☐ ☐ Western Europe (Germany, Austria, Italy, and all countries to the west, including the UK and Ireland)
☐ ☐ Northern Europe (Norway, Sweden, Finland, Iceland)
☐ ☐ Central and Southern Europe (The Czech Republic, Slovakia, Hungary, Romania, Bulgaria, ex-Yugoslavian countries, Greece)
☐ ☐ Eastern Europe (Lithuania, Latvia, Estonia, Byelorussia, Ukraine, Moldavia, the European part of Russia)
☐ ☐ Northern and Central Asia, including China
☐ ☐ Eastern Asia (Kamchatka, Sakhalin, North and South Korea, Japan)
☐ ☐ Middle East (Turkey and Iran and all other countries south of them; excepting Egypt and Sudan)
☐ Southern Asia (from Afghanistan to India and Nepal)
☐ Southeast Asia (from Bangladesh to Indonesia and the Philippines)
☐ North Africa (from Morocco to Egypt)
☐ Africa (all countries except for the 4 countries in the north of the continent)
☐ North America (USA and Canada)
☐ Central America, including Mexico and Panama
☐ South America
☐ Australia and Oceania

2. How long do you usually travel for?
☐ up to 2 weeks ☐ up to 1 month ☐ more than 1 month

3. How often do you go abroad on holidays?
☐ once a year ☐ twice a year ☐ more than twice a year

4. How do you travel?
☐ individually in groups of up to 4 people
☐ individually in groups of over 4 people
☐ in organised groups (package tours)
☐ in organised groups (hotel stay plus short excursions)
☐ in a different way (how?) ....

5. What means of transport do you usually use in your travels (you can choose more than one option)?

- [ ] train
- [ ] coach, minibus
- [ ] plane
- [ ] private car
- [ ] rented car
- [ ] other means of transport ....

- [ ] motorcycle / scooter
- [ ] bicycle
- [ ] ship
- [ ] sailboat
- [ ] kayak / pontoon / catamaran

6. What are the aims of your travels (you can choose more than one option)?

- [ ] learning about culture and art
- [ ] learning about and observing nature
- [ ] other – what? ....

- [ ] active relaxation
- [ ] sport achievements

7. Where do you stay during your travels?

- [ ] hostels
- [ ] guest rooms, cheap hotels
- [ ] private apartments of local people
- [ ] other places (what?) ....

- [ ] top-class hotels
- [ ] camping sites

8. Where do you seek information about the country or the region that you plan to visit?

- [ ] the Internet
- [ ] tourist and travellers' magazines
- [ ] friends
- [ ] other sources ....

- [ ] tourist guidebooks
- [ ] academic or popular books

9. Please list the titles of tourist magazines you regularly read and addresses of the websites that you regularly visit

....

....

PERSONAL INFORMATION

1. Name ....

2. Date of birth (dd – mm – yy) ....

3. Address for correspondence (street, house and flat number, postal code, town or city, province)

....

....

5. Telephone ....

6. e-mail address (if you have one) ....

7. Education:

- [ ] elementary
- [ ] secondary
- [ ] higher

8. Social-professional status:

- [ ] student
- [ ] teacher, academic
- [ ] free lance (self-employed e.g. doctor, lawyer, journalist, etc.)
- [ ] employed (e.g. office worker, clerk, economist, engineer, seller, etc.)
- [ ] businessperson (company owner), manager in a large company
- [ ] unemployed
- [ ] other professions

I agree that my personal information may be processed and used for promotional purposes by the Bezdroża company (according to the Act of 29 August, 1997 on the protection of personal information).

SIGNATURE: ....

Wydawnictwo Bezdroża
ul. Pychowicka 7, 30-364 Kraków, tel./fax: 012 /269 29 61
www.bezdroza.com, e-mail: biuro@bezdroza.com.pl